1 R BASICS

What is R?

R is both a programming language and an environment used in data analytics, statistical computing, and scientific research. It is amongst the best programming languages for researchers, data analysts, statisticians, and marketers. They use R to retrieve, clean, analyze, visualize and then present their data. Some of the reasons behind the increasing popularity in the use of R are an easy to use interface and more expressive syntax.

R is interpreted rather than being compiled. This means that we have the R interpreter. R is available for free under the GNU General Public License, and its pre-compiled binaries are available for various operating systems including Windows, Linux, and Mac OS. R was developed by Ross Ihaka and Robert Gentleman at the University of Auckland in New Zealand. The name R was derived from the first name of the two developers of the language, Ross and Robert.

R has been extensively used in performing data analysis tasks. This is because it is good for computing the various statistical measures from both small and huge sets of data. The language has numerous libraries that can be used for data processing. Other than that, R is a good tool for data visualization. It makes it easy for us to represent data using graphs and charts. This makes it easy for one to derive patterns, trends, and relationships from datasets.

R Environment Setup

Before you can begin to write and run your R programs, you need to install the R. We will guide you on how to install R in both Windows and Linux.

Installation on Windows

First, you need to download R and store it in one of your local directories. The R software for Windows can be downloaded from the following URL:

https://cran.r-project.org/bin/windows/base/

The download will come in an executable form (.exe), so you just have to double click it to launch the installation. During the installation, you can choose the default settings so that the process may be easy for you. For those using Windows 32-bit, only the 32-bit version will be installed, but for those using the 64-bit version, both the 32-bit and 64-bit versions will be installed.

Once the installation is completed, launch R from the Start button and then All Programs. You will be presented with the R console as shown below:

```
C:\Users\admin>Rscript hello.R
[1] "Hello World"

C:\Users\admin>
```

R Comments

Comments are the sections of code that the interpreter will skip or ignore. They are made for explanations so that one may know the meaning of various lines of code even if the cod was written by someone else. A comment may span a single line or multiple lines. To write a single-line comment, precede it with the pound (#) symbol as shown below:

```
helloString <- "Hello World"
# print text on the screen
print ( helloString)
```

The line preceded with the # symbol will be skipped or ignored by the R interpreter. If the comment spans more than one line, do a trick and enclose it within double or single quotes. For example:

```
helloString <- "Hello World"
"print text on the screen. This comment
spans more than one line"
print ( helloString)
```

R Programming

R is one of the best programming languages for statistics and data analysis. To start writing and running R, we need to install the R package on our computer. R codes can be executed directly on the R console or by creating a script file and executing it from there. To create a single-line comment, precede the line with the pound symbol (#). Ro writes a multi-line comment, enclose it within single or double quotes.

2 R DATA TYPES

In this chapter, we will discuss the various data types that R supports.

Variables are used to store information. They preserve memory locations for the purpose of storing values. When a variable is created, some space is reserved in the memory. You will often need to store information about different data types, including integer, floating point, Boolean, etc. This means that the data type of the variable matters. It determines the amount of memory allocated to the space and the kind of value that can be stored in the space.

In most programming languages such as C and Java, a variable is defined as a particular data type. This is not the case with R since the variables are assigned with R-objects, and the data type of the R-object will become the data type of the variable. There are different types of R-objects, but the common ones include the following:

- Vectors
- Matrices
- Lists

- Arrays
- Data Frames
- Factors

The vectors R-objects form the most basic data types in R and they hold elements of different classes.

Let us discuss the above R-objects one by one:

Vectors

A vector is simply a one-dimensional array. A vector can be created using any of the basic data types that you know. The vector should have elements of the same type. The simplest way for us to create a vector in R is by use of the c command. The command indicates that we have various elements that will be combined into a vector.

Here is an example:

```
# Create a vector.
student <- c('james','mark',"jane")
print(student)
# Get the class of our vector.
print(class(student))
```

The code should return the following result:

```
[1] "james" "mark"   "jane"
[1] "character"
```

We have created a vector named student with three elements. The class method has helped us know the class of the vector, which is the type of elements stored in the vector. From the output, we can say that the vector is storing character elements.

We can also create vectors holding elements of other data types. This is shown below:

```
vector1 <- c(1,2,5.3,6,-2,4) # a numeric
vector

vector2 <- c(TRUE,TRUE,TRUE,FALSE,TRUE,FALSE)
#a logical vector

print(vector1)

print(vector2)
```

The code will print the following:

```
[1]  1.0  2.0  5.3  6.0 -2.0  4.0
[1]  TRUE  TRUE  TRUE FALSE  TRUE FALSE
```

We have created a numeric and a logical vector.

We can access the elements of a vector using their indexes. The first element of the vector is kept at index 1, while the last element of the vector is kept at index n, where n is the total number of vector elements.

For example:

```
vector1 <- c(1,2,5.3,6,-2,4) # a numeric
vector
```

```
vector2 <- c(TRUE, TRUE, TRUE, FALSE, TRUE, FALSE)
#a logical vector

print(vector1[c(2,4)])# access 2nd and 4th
elements of the vector

print(vector2[c(1,4)]) # access 1st and 4th
elements of the vector
```

The code will return the following result:

```
[1] 2 6
[1] TRUE TRUE
```

We can use the: operator to create a vector of consecutive numbers. Here are simple examples:

```
v <- 1:8; v
```

The above will create a vector with numbers 1 to 8 as shown below:

```
> v <- 1:8; v
[1] 1 2 3 4 5 6 7 8
>
```

Here is another example:

```
v <- 2:-2; v
```

The code will return a vector of numbers going backwards, from 2 to -2 as shown below:

```
> v <- 2:-2; v
[1]  2  1  0 -1 -2
>
```

If you need to create a more complex sequence, you can use the seq() function. A good example is when you need to define the number of points in an interval, or the step size. Here are some examples:

```
seq(1, 3, by=0.2)          # define the step
size
```

It will return the following output:

```
> seq(1, 3, by=0.2)
[1] 1.0 1.2 1.4 1.6 1.8 2.0 2.2 2.4 2.6 2.8 3.0
>
```

We are printing numbers between 1 and 3 at intervals of 0.2 after each iteration.

Here is another example:

```
seq(1, 5, length.out=4)    # define the
vector length
```

The code will return the following:

```
> seq(1, 5, length.out=4)
[1] 1.000000 2.333333 3.666667 5.000000
>
```

It is possible for us to modify a vector, in which we will change the elements contained in it can be achieved by the use of the assignment operator. We can use the techniques for accessing the vector elements so as to modify them. For the purpose of truncating elements, we can use reassignments. Consider the following example:

Suppose we have the vector x with the following elements:

```
> x
[1] 1 3 2 4 5
>
```

Let us modify the 3rd element of the vector:

```
x[3] <- 0; x
```

So it should run as shown below:

```
> x[3] <- 0; x
[1] 1 3 0 4 5
>
```

The 3rd element has been changed from 2 to 0.
Let us modify all the vector elements that are less than 4:

14

```
x[x<4] <- 2; x
```

It should run as follows:

```
> x[x<4] <- 2; x
[1] 2 2 2 4 5
> |
```

All elements below 4 have been changed to 2s.

To delete a vector, we simply have to assign to it the value NULL. For example:

```
x <- NULL
```

This is demonstrated in the sequence of steps given below:

```
> x
[1] 2 2 2 4 5
> x <- NULL
> x
NULL
> |
```

Matrices

A matrix is a data set represented in a two-dimensional rectangular form. All the columns of the matrix should be of the same data type and the same length. It is similar to a vector, but it comes with the dimension attribute. To check the dimensions of an object, use the *attributes()* function.

To know whether an element is a matrix or not, we use the class attribute as shown below:

```
class(x)
```

```
> class(x)
[1] "NULL"
> |
```

The above output shows that x is not a matrix.

To create a matrix in R, we use a vector input to the matrix function. The following syntax demonstrates this:

```
my_matrix <- matrix(vector, nrow=r, ncol=c,
byrow=FALSE,

    dimnames=list(char_vector_rownames,
char_vector_colnames))
```

A *byRow=True* parameter indicates that the matrix should be filled by rows. *A byRow=FALSE* parameter indicates that the matrix should be filled by columns. The latter is used as the default. The dimnames will provide optional labels for both the rows and the columns. We should also pass the right value to the nrow and ncol arguments. It is not necessary for us to pass values for both the nrow and ncol arguments. If you pass a value for one of these, the value of the other one will be inferred from the length of the data.

Here is an example:

```
# Create a matrix.
M = matrix( c('x','x','y','z','y','x'), nrow
= 2, ncol = 3, byrow = TRUE)
print(M)
```

R Programming

The program should give you the following output:

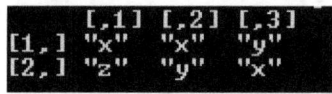

Here is another example:

```
matrix(1:12, nrow = 4, ncol = 3)
```

This generates the following matrix:

```
> matrix(1:12, nrow = 4, ncol = 3)
     [,1] [,2] [,3]
[1,]    1    5    9
[2,]    2    6   10
[3,]    3    7   11
[4,]    4    8   12
>
```

We can modify it to the following:

```
matrix(1:12, .nrow = 4)
```

```
> matrix(1:12, nrow = 4)
     [,1] [,2] [,3]
[1,]    1    5    9
[2,]    2    6   10
[3,]    3    7   11
[4,]    4    8   12
>
```

Even though we omitted the *ncol* attribute, the same matrix has been generated.

The numbers have been filled by columns. If we need them to be filled by row, we can set the *byrow* property to TRUE as in our first example. This is demonstrated below:

```
matrix(1:12, nrow=3, byrow=TRUE)
```

This will return the following:

```
> matrix(1:12, nrow=3, byrow=TRUE)
     [,1] [,2] [,3] [,4]
[1,]    1    2    3    4
[2,]    5    6    7    8
[3,]    9   10   11   12
>
```

Yes, you may fill the matrix row-wise, but internally, the matrix is stored in column-major order.

We can assign names to the columns of the matrix during the creation of the matrix. We only have to pass a 2 element list to the *dimnames* argument. Consider the example given below:

R Programming

```
x <- matrix(1:12, nrow = 4, dimnames =
list(c("W","X","Y" ,"Z"), c("A","B","C")))
```

The code should return the following:

```
> x <- matrix(1:12, nrow = 4, dimnames = list(c("W","X","Y" ,"Z"), c("A","B","C")))
> x
  A B  C
W 1 5  9
X 2 6 10
Y 3 7 11
Z 4 8 12
> |
```

To change or access the names, we can use two helpful functions, the *colnames()* and *rownames()* functions. The name of the matrix should be passed to the function as the argument. For example:

```
colnames(x)
```

```
> colnames(x)
[1] "A" "B" "C"
> |
```

The names of the columns have been defined. Let us see the names of the rows:

```
rownames(x)
```

```
> rownames(x)
[1] "W" "X" "Y" "Z"
> |
```

The names of the matrix rows have been returned.

We can also create a matrix by use of the *cbind()* and *rbind()* functions for column bind and row bind respectively. Let us give examples of these:

```
cbind(c(1, 6, 9),c(3, 5, 8))
```

```
> cbind(c(1, 6, 9),c(3, 5, 8))
     [,1] [,2]
[1,]    1    3
[2,]    6    5
[3,]    9    8
> |
```

The matrix has been created.

```
rbind(c(1, 6, 9),c(3, 5, 8))
```

```
> rbind(c(1, 6, 9),c(3, 5, 8))
     [,1] [,2] [,3]
[1,]    1    6    9
[2,]    3    5    8
> |
```

The matrix has been created.

The elements of a matrix can be accessed by use of a square bracket [indexing method. We can access the elements using the format *var[row, column]*, where the *rows* and column are vectors. R allows us to specify the row numbers and column numbers as vectors then use it for indexing. If any of the fields inside the brackets are found blank, all will be selected. To specify the rows and columns that are to be executed, we can use negative integers. Consider the example given below.

First, let us create a matrix from a vector:

```
x <- c(1, 3, 6, 4, 5, 0)
dim(x) <- c(2, 3)
```

```
> x <- c(1, 3, 6, 4, 5, 0)
> dim(x) <- c(2,3)
> x
     [,1] [,2] [,3]
[1,]    1    6    5
[2,]    3    4    0
>
```

Here, we need to access the rows 1 and 2 and columns 2 and 3 of the matrix x:

```
x[c(1, 2),c(2, 3)]
```

The above will return the following:

```
> x[c(1,2),c(2,3)]
     [,1] [,2]
[1,]    6    5
[2,]    4    0
>
```

If the column space is left blank, then the entire columns will be selected as shown below:

```
x[c(1, 2),]
```

The command will return the following:

```
> x[c(1, 2),]
     [,1] [,2] [,3]
[1,]   1    6    5
[2,]   3    4    0
>
```

If the row and column fields are left empty, the entire matrix will be selected:

```
x[,]
```

This will return the following:

```
> x[,]
     [,1] [,2] [,3]
[1,]   1    6    5
[2,]   3    4    0
>
```

We can select all rows except the first one:

```
> x[-1,]
[1] 3 4 0
>
```

Note that after indexing, if the matrix returns a row matrix or column matrix, the displayed result is a vector. You can see this by running the following commands:

```
x[1,]
class(x[1,])
```

The commands will run as follows:

```
> x[1,]
[1] 1 6 5
> class(x[1,])
[1] "numeric"
> |
```

To prevent this behavior from occurring, we can use the attribute *drop* = *FALSE* when indexing. This is demonstrated below:

```
x[1,,drop=FALSE]
```

The command will return the following:

```
> x[1,,drop=FALSE]
     [,1] [,2] [,3]
[1,]    1    6    5
> |
```

The output shown above is a matrix rather than a vector. You can confirm this by running the following command:

```
class(x[1,,drop=FALSE])
```

It should run as follows:

```
> class(x[1,,drop=FALSE])
[1] "matrix"
>
```

We can index a matrix using a single vector. When we index in that way, it will act like a vector that has been formed by stacking the matrix columns one after another. The result will be a vector.

This is demonstrated below:

```
> x

> x[1:4]

> x[c(3,5,7)]
```

The commands will execute as shown below:

```
> x
       [,1] [,2] [,3]
[1,]     1    6    5
[2,]     3    4    0
> x[1:4]
[1] 1 3 6 4
> x[c(3,5,7)]
[1]   6   5  NA
>
```

Whenever you need to modify the elements of a matrix, you can use the necessary methods to access the elements and change them as required. Suppose we have the following matrix x:

```
> x
      [,1] [,2] [,3]
[1,]    1    6    5
[2,]    3    4    0
> |
```

We can modify a single as shown below:

```
x[2,2] <- 10; x
```

The command should execute as follows:

```
> x[2,2] <- 10; x
      [,1] [,2] [,3]
[1,]    1    6    5
[2,]    3   10    0
> |
```

Let us modify all the elements that are less than 5:

```
x[x<5] <- 0; x
```

The command should return the following:

```
> x[x<5] <- 0; x
      [,1] [,2] [,3]
[1,]    0    6    5
[2,]    0   10    0
```

We can use the rbind() and cbind() methods to add a row and a column respectively. We can also remove it through reassignment. Here is how we can add a column:

```
cbind(x, c(1, 3, 6))
```

Here is how we can add a row:

```
rbind(x,c(1,2,3))
```

Lists

A list is an R-object which can be used for holding a number of different elements inside it. This means that a list may hold together elements that are not related. Examples of such elements include functions, vectors, and even other lists.

Consider the example given below:

```
# Create a list.
mylist <- list(c(1,2,3),22.4,sin)
# Print the list.
print(mylist)
```

The program will give you the output shown below:

```
[[1]]
[1] 1 2 3

[[2]]
[1] 22.4

[[3]]
function (x)  .Primitive("sin")
```

To know whether it is a list, we can use the typeof() function.

```
typeof(mylist)
```

The command will run as follows:

```
> typeof(mylist)
[1] "list"
>
```

To know the number of elements stored in the list, we can call the *length()* function:

```
length(mylist)
```

The command should run as shown below:

```
> length(mylist)
[1] 3
>
```

To change an element of a list, we can use reassignment. This is demonstrated below:

```
x[[6]] <- 8; x
```

The command will run as follows:

```
> x[[6]] <- 8; x
      [,1] [,2] [,3]
[1,]    0    6    5
[2,]    0   10    8
> |
```

0 has been replaced with 8. It is the 6th element of the list.

Arrays

An R matrix must be of two dimensions, but an array can be of any dimensions. The array attribute takes the "dim" attribute which specifies the number of dimensions that you want to create for the array. Consider the example given below in which we will create a two-dimensional array:

```
# Create an array.
x <- array(c('boy', 'girl'),dim = c(3,3,2))
print(x)
```

The program should give you the output given below:

```
, , 1

      [,1]    [,2]    [,3]
[1,]  "boy"   "girl"  "boy"
[2,]  "girl"  "boy"   "girl"
[3,]  "boy"   "girl"  "boy"

, , 2

      [,1]    [,2]    [,3]
[1,]  "girl"  "boy"   "girl"
[2,]  "boy"   "girl"  "boy"
[3,]  "girl"  "boy"   "girl"
```

Data Frames

Data frames are simply tabular data objects. It is possible for you to have data of different data types in the different columns of the data frame, which is not allowed in a matrix. The first column of the data frame can be numeric, the second can contain logical values, the third column can have characters, etc. It is simply a list of vectors of an equal length. Note that the data frame is a two dimensional object.

In R, a data frame can be created by calling the *data.frame()* function. To know whether an element is a data frame or not, just call the *class()* method. Let us begin by creating a data frame x:

```r
x <- data.frame("SN" = 1:2, "Age" = c(22,
14), "Name" = c("Alice", "John"))
```

We can then view the structure of the data frame as follows:

```r
str(x)
```

R Programming

The commands should execute as follows:

```
> x <- data.frame("SN" = 1:2, "Age" = c(22, 14), "Name" = c("Alice", "John"))
> str(x)
'data.frame':   2 obs. of  3 variables:
 $ SN  : int  1 2
 $ Age : num  22 14
 $ Name: Factor w/ 2 levels "Alice","John": 1 2
>
```

We can also view how the elements are arranged within the data frame:

```
> x
  SN Age  Name
1  1  22 Alice
2  2  14  John
>
```

In the above data frame, the third column, which is Name, is a *factor*, instead of being a character vector. By default, the *data.frame()* function will convert a character factor into a vector. This behavior can be suppressed by using the attribute *stringAsFactors=FALSE*.

This is shown below:

```
x <- data.frame("SN" = 1:2, "Age" = c(22,
14), "Name" = c("Alice", "John"),
stringsAsFactors = FALSE)
```

We can then then look at the structure of the data frame:

```
str(x)
```

The two commands will execute as follows:

```
> x <- data.frame("SN" = 1:2, "Age" = c(22, 14), "Name" = c("Alice", "John"), stringsAsFactors = FALSE)
> str(x)
'data.frame':   2 obs. of  3 variables:
 $ SN  : int  1 2
 $ Age :| num  22 14
 $ Name: chr  "Alice" "John"
> |
```

The third column is now a character vector. Majority of input functions provided by R such as read.csv(), read.table() etc. also read the data into a data frame.

We can access the elements of a data frame in the same way that we access the elements of a matrix or a list.

To access the elements of a data frame as a list, we can use the [, [[or $ operators, and we will be able to access the columns of the data frame. To access the Name column of data frame x, we can run the following command on the terminal:

```
x["Name"]
```

It will return the following output:

```
> x["Name"]
    Name
1 Alice
2  John
> |
```

We can also access the same as follows:

```
x$Name
```

It will return the following output:

```
> x$Name
[1] "Alice" "John"
>
```

The same can also be accessed as follows:

```
x[["Name"]]
```

It returns the following:

```
> x[["Name"]]
[1] "Alice" "John"
>
```

It is also possible for us to access data frames as matrices. To achieve this, we have to provide the indexes of the row and column of the element we need to access.

R comes with a set of inbuilt datasets. We will use one of them for this section. We will use *trees* dataset. The dataset shows the Girth, the Height and the Volume of Black Cherry trees. We can examine the data frame using the *str()* and *head()* functions. This is shown below:

```
str(trees)
```

Which returns the following?

```
> str(trees)
'data.frame':   31 obs. of  3 variables:
 $ Girth : num  8.3 8.6 8.8 10.5 10.7 10.8 11 11 11.1 11.2 ...
 $ Height: num  70 65 63 72 81 83 66 75 80 75 ...
 $ Volume: num  10.3 10.3 10.2 16.4 18.8 19.7 15.6 18.2 22.6 19.9 ...
> |
```

Let us view the first 5 rows of the dataset:

```
head(trees, n=5)
```

The command will return the following output:

```
> head(trees, n=5)
  Girth Height Volume
1   8.3     70   10.3
2   8.6     65   10.3
3   8.8     63   10.2
4  10.5     72   16.4
5  10.7     81   18.8
> |
```

The dataset has 31 rows and 3 columns. Let us now try to access the data frame as a matrix. First, let us select and return the 1st and the 3rd rows only:

```
trees[1:3,]
```

This should return the following:

```
> trees[1:3,]
  Girth Height  Volume
1   8.3      70    10.3
2   8.6      65    10.3
3   8.8      63    10.2
> |
```

Let us select all the rows in which the Height is great than 82:

```
trees[trees$Height > 82,]
```

The command will return the following:

```
> trees[trees$Height > 82,]
   Girth Height  Volume
6   10.8      83    19.7
17  12.9      85    33.8
18  13.3      86    27.4
31  20.6      87    77.0
> |
```

To modify the elements of a data frame, just use reassignment in the same way we did for matrices.

Suppose the following data frame x:

```
> x
  SN Age   Name
1  1  22  Alice
2  2  14   John
> |
```

Let us now change the value of age for Alice from 22 to 23:

```
x[1,"Age"] <- 23; x
```

The code will return the following result:

```
> x[1,"Age"] <- 23; x
  SN Age  Name
1  1  23 Alice
2  2  14  John
>
```

To add a new row to a data frame, use the rbind() function as shown below:

```
rbind(x,list(1, 20,"Paul"))
```

You should now have the following data frame:

```
> rbind(x,list(1, 20,"Paul"))
  SN Age  Name
1  1  23 Alice
2  2  14  John
3  1  20  Paul
>
```

Similarly, if you need to add a new column, use the *cbind()* function:

```
cbind(x, Course=c("Eng.","IT"))
```

The command should run as follows:

```
> cbind(x, Course=c("Eng.","IT"))
  SN Age  Name Course
1  1  23 Alice   Eng.
2  2  14  John     IT
>
```

Since the data frames are implemented as lists, one can add new columns to the data frame using list-like assignments. For example:

```
x$Course <- c("Eng.","IT"); x
```

The code will return the following result:

```
> x$Course <- c("Eng.","IT"); x
  SN Age  Name Course
1  1  23 Alice   Eng.
2  2  14  John     IT
>
```

To delete a data frame column, just assign a value of NULL to it. Let us delete the Course column from data frame x:

```
x$Course <- NULL
```

The command should run and return the following output:

```
> x$Course <- NULL
> x
  SN Age  Name
1  1  23 Alice
2  2  14  John
>
```

The Course column has been dropped successfully. Similarly, to delete the rows of a data frame, we can use reassignments. This is demonstrated below:

```
x <- x[-1,]
```

This will run as shown below:

```
> x <- x[-1,]
> x
  SN Age Name
2  2  14 John
> |
```

Factors

Factors are data objects used for the purpose of categorizing data and then storing them under levels. They can be used for storage of both strings and integers. Factors are only useful in the columns with a limited number of unique values. They are good in data analysis and statistical modeling.

For us to create factors in R, we use the factor() method and use a vector as the input. Consider the example given below showing how this function can be used:

```
d <-
c("East","West","East","North","North","East"
,"West","West","West","East","North")
```

Let us now see the contents of the vector:

```
> d <- c("East","West","East","North","North","East","West","West","West","East","North")
> d
 [1] "East"   "West"   "East"   "North"  "North"  "East"   "West"   "West"   "West"
[10] "East"   "North"
> |
```

To check whether d is a factor or not, we use the *is.factor()* attribute as shown below:

```
is.factor(d)
```

The script returns the following:

```
> is.factor(d)
[1] FALSE
> |
```

Object d is not a factor. It is a vector. We need to call the *factor()* method and pass the name of the vector to it. The vector will be changed to a factor:

```
# Applying the factor function.
factor_data <- factor(d)
```

Let us need the contents of the factor and determine whether d is a factor or not:

```
is.factor(factor_data)
```

Execution of the program should give the following output:

```
> factor_data <- factor(d)
> d
 [1] "East"  "West"  "East"  "North" "North" "East"  "West"  "West"  "West"  "East"  "North"
> is.factor(factor_data)
[1] TRUE
> |
```

The output shows that we already have a factor. We have successfully created a factor from a vector by calling the *factor()* method.

We can also create a factor from a data frame. Once you have created a data frame having a column of text data, R treats the next column as categorical data and then creates factors on it. Consider the example given below showing how this can be done:

```
# Creating the vectors for the data frame.
height <- c(140,152,164,137,166,157,112)
weight <- c(38,49,76,54,97,22,30)
gender <-
c("male","male","female","female","male","fem
ale","male")

# Creating the data frame.
input_data <-
data.frame(height,weight,gender)
```

Let us view the contents of the data frame:

```
> height <- c(140,152,164,137,166,157,112)
> weight <- c(38,49,76,54,97,22,30)
> gender <- c("male","male","female","female","male","female","male")
> input_data <- data.frame(height,weight,gender)
> input_data
  height weight gender
1    140     38   male
2    152     49   male
3    164     76 female
4    137     54 female
5    166     97   male
6    157     22 female
7    112     30   male
> |
```

Let us check whether the column gender is a factor or not:

```
is.factor(input_data$gender)
```

It returns the following output:

```
> is.factor(input_data$gender)
[1] TRUE
> |
```

Yes, the column is a factor.

We can now print the gender column to see the levels:

```
input_data$gender
```

The script will return the following output:

```
> input_data$gender
[1] male    male    female female male    female male
Levels: female male
> |
```

The order of the levels contained in a factor can be changed by applying the factor function again while specifying the new order of the levels. Consider the example given below:

```
d <-
c("East","West","East","North","North","East"
,"West","West","West","East","North")
```

Let us create the factors:

```
factor_data <- factor(d)
```

Let us display the factor data:

```
> factor_data
 [1] East  West  East  North North East  West  West  West  East  North
Levels: East North West
>
```

Let us now apply the factor function and the required order for the level:

```
new_order_data <- factor(factor_data,levels =
c("East","West","North"))
```

Let us view the data:

```
> new_order_data <- factor(factor_data,levels = c("East","West","North"))
> new_order_data
 [1] East  West  East  North North East  West  West  West  East  North
Levels: East West North
>
```

In R, we can generate factor levels using the "gl()" function. The function will take two integers, in which the first integer will specify the number of levels while the second integer will specify the number of times for each level. The function takes the syntax given below:

```
gl(n, k, labels)
```

The following parameters have been used in the above syntax:
- **n**- this is an integer which defines the number of levels.
- **k**- this is an integer which specifies the number of replications.
- **labels**- this is a vector of labels representing the resulting factor levels.

Consider the example given below which shows how the function can be used:

```
vec <- gl(2, 3, labels = c("Texas",
"Seattle","Boston"))
```

Then we print the contents of the vector:

```
> vec
[1] Texas   Texas   Texas   Seattle Seattle Seattle
Levels: Texas Seattle Boston
>
```

We can also create a factor directly from the *factor()* function. The following example demonstrates this:

42

```
x <- factor(c("Married", "married", "single",
"single"));
```

We can then print out the contents of the factor:

```
> x <- factor(c("Married", "married", "single", "single"));
> x
[1] Married married single  single
Levels: married Married single
>
```

The elements of a factor can be accessed in the same way as those of a vector. For example:

Here is our factor **x:**

```
> x
[1] Married married single  single
Levels: married Married single
>
```

Let us access the 2nd element of the factor:

```
x[2]
```

The script will run as follows:

```
> x[2]
[1] married
Levels: married Married single
>
```

Let us access the 1st and the 3rd elements of the factor:

```
x[c(1, 3)]
```

It will return the following:

```
> x[c(1, 3)]
[1] Married single
Levels: married Married single
> |
```

Let us access all the factor elements except the 1st one:

```
x[-1]
```

It prints the following output:

```
> x[-1]
[1] married single  single
Levels: married Married single
> |
```

To modify the elements of a vector, we only have to use simple reassignments. However, it's impossible for us to choose components outside its predefined levels. Here is an example:

```
x[3] <- "married"
```

What we have done is that we have changed the value of the 3rd element from single to married. The code should run as follows:

```
> x[3] <- "married"
> x
[1] Married married married single
Levels: married Married single
>
```

The above output shows that the change was made successfully. In our case, we only have two levels, married and single. If we attempt to assign a value that is outside this, we will get a warning message. Here is an example:

```
x[3] <- "divorced"
```

This will run as shown below:

```
> x[3] <- "divorced"
Warning message:
In `[<-.factor`(`*tmp*`, 3, value = "divorced") :
  invalid factor level, NA generated
```

Strings

In R, strings are written within single or double quotes. Although we are allowed to use single quotes for declaration of a string in R, these are internally stored with double quotes. If you have started and ended with single quotes, it is possible for you to insert double quotes within the string. The same case applies to a string which starts and ends with single quotes, as you are allowed to insert single quotes within. Even though that is true, you are not allowed to insert double quotes inside a string which starts and ends with double quotes. The same case applies when you are using single quotes.

Consider the example given below which shows how these can be used:

```
w <- 'Begin and end with a single quote'
```

The string will be created. Let us print it:

```
> w <- 'Begin and end with a single quote'
> w
[1] "Begin and end with a single quote"
>
```

```
x <- "Begin and end with the double quotes"
```

Let us print the string:

```
> x <- "Begin and end with the double quotes"
> x
[1] "Begin and end with the double quotes"
>
```

Here are other examples:

```
y <- "single quote ' added in between the double quotes"
```

```
> y <- "single quote ' added in between the double quotes"
> y
[1] "single quote ' added in between the double quotes"
>
```

```
z <- 'Double quotes " added in between sa
ingle quote'
```

```
> z <- 'Double quotes " added in between sa ingle quote'
> z
[1] "Double quotes \" added in between sa ingle quote"
>
```

We can concatenate R strings using the *paste()* function. The function can take any number of arguments that you need to concatenate. Here is the syntax for the function:

```
paste(..., sep = " ", collapse = NULL)
```

The *"..."* represents the number of arguments that are to be combined or concatenated. The *"sep"* represents any separator between the arguments, but this one is optional. The *"collapse"* eliminates any space in the two strings. However, this is not the space existing between any two words of a string.

Consider the example given below:

```
x <- "Hi"

y <- 'How'

z <- "was your day?"

paste(x,y,z)
```

This returns the following:

```
> x <- "Hi"
> y <- 'How'
> z <- "was your day?"
> paste(x,y,z)
[1] "Hi How was your day?"
>
```

```
paste(x,y,z, sep = "-")
```

Returns the following:

```
> paste(x,y,z, sep = "-")
[1] "Hi-How-was your day?"
>
```

```
paste(x,y,z, sep = "", collapse = "")
```

It returns the following:

```
> paste(x,y,z, sep = "", collapse = "")
[1] "HiHowwas your day?"
>
```

It is possible for us to count the number of characters a string has. We use the nchar() function for this. The function will count the number of characters contained in the string including the white spaces. It takes the basic syntax given below:

```
nchar(x)
```

In which the x is a vector input.

Consider the example given below:

```
result <- nchar("Counting number of
characters")
```

The above will return the following:

```
> result <- nchar("Counting number of characters")
> result
[1] 29
>
```

The string has a total of 29 characters including the white spaces.

We can play around with strings by changing the case, that is, from uppercase to lowercase and vice versa. Here are the functions for doing this:

```
toupper(x)
tolower(x)
```

In which the x is a vector input. Consider the example given below showing how these two functions can be used:

Let us change a string to Upper case:

```
result <- toupper("This is To Be Changed To
UpperCase")
```

This will return the following:

```
> result <- toupper("This is To Be Changed To UpperCase")
> result
[1] "THIS IS TO BE CHANGED TO UPPERCASE"
> |
```

Let us change a string from uppercase to lowercase:

```
result <- tolower("This is To Be Changed To
Lowercase")
```

The script will return the following:

```
> result <- tolower("This is To Be Changed To Lowercase")
> result
[1] "this is to be changed to lowercase"
> |
```

It is also possible for us to extract parts of a string. We use the *substring()* function with the following syntax:

```
substring(x, first, last)
```

The following parameters have been used in the above syntax:
- **x**- this represents the character vector input.

- **first**- this represents the position of the first character which is to be extracted.

- **last**- this is the position of the last character which is to be extracted.

Consider the example given below:

We will extract characters of a string from the 4th to the 6th position:

```
result <- substring("Nicholas", 4, 6)
```

The script will return the following output:

```
> result <- substring("Nicholas", 4, 6)
> result
[1] "hol"
>
```

There are different data types supported in R.

- A vector is an R-object that stores elements of the same type. It is simply a one-dimensional array. We can access and modify the elements stored in a vector.

- A matrix is a data set represented in a two-dimensional rectangular form. All the columns of the matrix should be of the same data type and the same length. The elements of a matrix can be accessed and modified.

- A list is an R-object which can be used for holding a number of different elements inside it. This means that a list may hold together elements that are not related, that is, the elements must not belong to the same data type.

- In R, a matrix takes only one dimension, but an array can take many dimensions. The dim attribute is used to specify the number of dimensions of the array.

- A data frame represents data in a tabular form. The different columns of the data frame can have elements of different data types.

- R factors categorize data into different levels. The elements contained in a factor can be integers or strings. We can access and modify the elements of a vector.

- R strings should be enclosed within single or double quotes.

3 R VARIABLES AND CONSTANTS

Variables are used for storage of data, whose value can change based on our need. Each R variable is given a unique name, and this is called the identifier. Here are the rules that govern the writing of identifiers in R:

- An identifier can have a combination of letters, digits, *period (.)* and *underscore (_).*
- The identifier must begin with either a letter or a period. If the identifier begins with a period, then it cannot be followed by a digit.
- The reserved R keywords cannot be used as identifiers.

Here are examples of valid identifiers in R:

```
name, Sum, .okay.with.dot, this_is_acceptad,
Position5
```

Here are examples of invalid identifiers in R:

```
pos@1, 5ex, _fine, TRUE, .One
```

In the earlier versions of R, the *underscore (_)* was used as an assignment operator. The *period(.)* was highly used in the names of variables with multiple words.

Today, R versions allow the use of underscore as a valid identifier but it is recommended that you use the period to separate words. For example, it is recommended that you use *my.variable* instead of *my_variable*. Alternatively, you can use the camel case, for example, *myVariable*.

Variable Assignment

The leftward, rightward and equal operators can be used for assigning values to variables. To print the value of the variable, you can use the *"print()"* or the *"cat()"* function. The *"cat()"* function will combine the multiple items so as to get a continuous output. Consider the example given below:

Let us use the equal operator for variable assignment:

```
var.1 = c(5,6,7,8)
```

Let us use the leftward operator for assignment:

```
var.2 <- c("learn programming in","R")
```

Let us use the rightward operator for assignment:
```
c(TRUE,1) -> var.3
```

We can then print the values of the variables:

```
> var.1 = c(5,6,7,8)
> var.2 <- c("learn programming in","R")
> c(TRUE,1) -> var.3
> var.1
[1] 5 6 7 8
> var.2
[1] "learn programming in" "R"
> var.3
[1] 1 1
>
```

Those are the three ways through which we can assign values to variables in R.

Data Type for a Variable

In R, a variable is not declared to be of a particular data type. what happens is that it will get the data type of the R object already assigned to it. This is why R is a dynamically typed language, meaning that the data type of the variable can be changed again and again in our program. Type the following program in an R script file and run it from the command prompt of your operating system:

```
var_y <- "Hello"
cat("The class for var_y is
",class(var_y),"\n")
var_y <- 34.5
```

```
cat(" At this point, the class for var_y is
",class(var_y),"\n")

var_x <- 27L

cat(" Lastly, the class for var_y becomes
",class(var_y),"\n")
```

The program will give the following output after execution:

```
The class for var_y is   character
  At this point, the class for var_y is   numeric
  Lastly, the class for var_y becomes   numeric
```

Finding Variables

To find all the variables that are contained in your workspace, you can use the *ls()* function. It can also be used with patterns for the purpose of matching the names of variables. This is shown below:

```
ls()
```

When running on the R console it will return the following:

```
> ls()
 [1] "a"          "b"          "my_comparisons" "ourcomparisons"
 [5] "pi"         "plot1"      "plot2"          "rel"
 [9] "relation"   "val"        "var.1"          "var.2"
[13] "var.3"      "weight"     "x"              "y"
> |
```

The script has returned all the variables that have been defined in the current workspace. If you have none, then nothing will be returned. Also, the variables have to match the ones you have defined within your programming environment.

The command can be used as follows with patterns:

To see all the variables whose identifiers, begin with pattern *"var"*:

```
ls(pattern = "var")
```

The script returns the following:

```
> ls(pattern = "var")
[1] "var.1" "var.2" "var.3"
> |
```

Deleting Variables

To remove a variable, we can use the *rm()* function. Suppose we need to delete a variable with the name *"var.2"*. We only have to invoke the *rm()* function and pass the name of the variable to it as the argument. This is demonstrated below:

```
rm(var.2)
```

```
> var.2
[1] "learn programming in" "R"
> rm(var.2)
> var.2
Error: object 'var.2' not found
> |
```

The variable was present in our workspace, but it was deleted after running the *rm()* function.

If we need to delete all the variables contained in the current workspace, we can use both the *rm()* and *ls()* functions at once. Let us demonstrate this:

```
rm(list = ls())

ls()
```

```
> ls()
 [1] "a"               "b"          "my_comparisons"  "ourcomparisons"
 [5] "pi"              "plot1"      "plot2"           "rel"
 [9] "relation"        "val"        "var.1"           "var.3"
[13] "weight"          "x"          "y"
> rm(list = ls())
> ls()
character(0)
> |
```

The output from the *ls()* function shows that all variables have been deleted from the workspace.

R supports the creation and use of constants. The value of a constant cannot be changed, just as the name suggests. R supports numeric and character constants. Let us discuss these:

Numeric Constants

All numbers fall under numeric constants. They can take a data type of integer, double or complex. To check this, we use the *typeof()* function. A numeric constant followed by an L is treated as an integer while a numeric constant followed by an i is treated as a complex. Here are examples that demonstrate this:

```
typeof(10)
```

```
typeof(8L)

typeof(7i)
```

These run as shown below:

```
> typeof(10)
[1] "double"
> typeof(8L)
[1] "integer"
> typeof(7i)
[1] "complex"
>
```

Character Constants

To create character constants, we use either single (') or double (") quotes as delimiters. Here are examples:

```
'john'

typeof("10")
```

These will run as shown below:

```
> 'john'
[1] "john"
> typeof("10")
[1] "character"
>
```

Built-in Constants

R also comes with a number of built-in constants. These are shown below together with their values:

```
> LETTERS
 [1] "A" "B" "C" "D" "E" "F" "G" "H" "I" "J" "K" "L" "M" "N" "O" "P" "Q" "R" "S"
[20] "T" "U" "V" "W" "X" "Y" "Z"
> letters
 [1] "a" "b" "c" "d" "e" "f" "g" "h" "i" "j" "k" "l" "m" "n" "o" "p" "q" "r" "s"
[20] "t" "u" "v" "w" "x" "y" "z"
> pi
[1] 3.141593
> month.name
 [1] "January"   "February"  "March"     "April"     "May"       "June"
 [7] "July"      "August"    "September" "October"   "November"  "December"
> month.abb
 [1] "Jan" "Feb" "Mar" "Apr" "May" "Jun" "Jul" "Aug" "Sep" "Oct" "Nov" "Dec"
>
```

However, you have to note that the above constants are declared as variables and it is possible for us to change their values. For example, we can change the value of the pie constant as shown below:

```
> pi
[1] 3.141593
> pi <- 12
> pi
[1] 12
>
```

The above shows that it is not good for us to rely on the built-in constants.

Getting User Input

To allow users to enter the input data, you can call the *readline()* function. This function reads data from the user and stores it in a variable. We can then access the data through that variable. Let us create an example that demonstrates how this can be done:

```
name <- readline(prompt="Enter your name: ")
age <- readline(prompt="Enter your age: ")
# convert the character to an integer
age <- as.integer(age)
print(paste("Hi,", name, "next year you will
be", age+1, "years old."))
```

The script will run as follows:

```
> name <- readline(prompt="Enter your name: ")
Enter your name: John
> age <- readline(prompt="Enter your age: ")
Enter your age: 12
> age <- as.integer(age)
> print(paste("Hi,", name, "next year you will be", age+1, "years old."))
[1] "Hi, John next year you will be 13 years old."
```

The user was prompted to enter values for both the name and age.

- A variable is used for the storage of values. The value of a variable can be changed.

- Each variable is assigned a unique name known as the identifier.

- The data type of a variable determines the type of data that can be stored in that variable.

- When you declare a variable, it is kept in the workspace. You can view all variables in the workspace by running the *ls()* function.

- To delete a variable from the workspace, we use the *rm()* function.

The *readline()* function helps us get input from users.

4 R OPERATORS

In this chapter, you will learn the various operators provided by r for performing different types of operations, including arithmetic, logical and bitwise operations.

In R, an operator is a symbol that instructs the interpreter to perform a certain mathematical or logical operation. R comes with several built-in operators that you can use for such tasks. R operators are classified as follows:

- Arithmetic Operators
- Relational Operators
- Logical Operators
- Assignment Operators

Arithmetic Operators

These are the types of operators used to perform mathematical operations like, addition, subtraction, division etc. Here are the various arithmetic operators provided by R and the tasks we use them for:

- \+ :Addition
- \- :Subtraction
- * :Multiplication
- / :Division
- ^ :Exponent
- %% :Modulus (Remainder from division)
- %/% :Integer Division

Let us run the following set of scripts to demonstrate how the above operators can be used in R:

```r
x <- 5
y <- 21
cat("x + y returns: ",x+y,"\n")
cat("x - y returns: ",x-y,"\n")
cat("x * y returns: ",x*y,"\n")
cat("x / y returns: ",x/y,"\n")
cat("y %/% x returns: ",y%/%x,"\n")
cat("y %% x returns: ",y%%x,"\n")
cat("y ^ x returns: ",y^x)
```

Just create an R script file and write the code there. Run it on the command prompt of your OS by invoking the Rscript interpreter. It will return the following:

```
x + y returns:    26
x - y returns:    -16
x * y returns:    105
x / y returns:    0.2380952
y %/% x returns:   4
y %% x returns:   1
y ^ x returns:    4084101
```

Relational Operators

Relational operators help us make comparisons between values. Here is the list of operators supported in R:

- < :Less than
- > :Greater than
- <=   :Less than or equal to
- >=   :Greater than or equal to
- ==   :Equal to
- !=   :Not equal to

Consider the following example:

```
x <- 5
y <- 21
cat("x < y is: ",x<y,"\n")
cat("x > y is: ",x>y,"\n")
cat("x <= 5 is: ",x<=5,"\n")
cat("y >= 20 is: ",y>=20,"\n")
cat("y == 16 is: ",y==16,"\n")
cat("x != 5 is: ",x!=5)
```

Write the script in an R script file and execute it from the command prompt of your OS. It will return the following output:

```
x < y is:    TRUE
x > y is:    FALSE
x <= 5 is:   TRUE
y >= 20 is:  TRUE
y == 16 is:  FALSE
x != 5 is:   FALSE
```

Logical Operators

We use these operators to perform Boolean operations such as AND, OR etc. Logical operators are only applicable to numeric, logical or complex vectors. Here are the logical operators supported by R:

- !: Logical NOT
- & :Element-wise logical AND
- && :Logical AND
- | :Element-wise logical OR
- || :Logical OR

The & and | operators perform an element-wise operation to give a result having the length of the longer operand. The && and || will examine only the first element of the operands and returns a single length logical vector. Zero is considered to be FALSE while non-zero numbers are treated as TRUE. The following example demonstrates how to use logical operators in R:

```
x <- c(TRUE, FALSE, 0, 7)
y <- c(FALSE, TRUE, FALSE, TRUE)
cat("!x returns: ",!x,"\n")
```

```
cat("x&y returns: ",x&y,"\n")
cat("x&&y returns: ",x&&y,"\n")
cat("x|y returns: ",x|y,"\n")
cat("x||y returns: ",x||y,"\n")
```

Write the script in an R script file and run it on the terminal of your OS. It will return the following result:

```
!x returns:    FALSE TRUE TRUE FALSE
x&y returns:   FALSE FALSE FALSE TRUE
x&&y returns:  FALSE
x|y returns:   TRUE TRUE FALSE TRUE
x||y returns:  TRUE
```

The ! x reversed the values stored in *x*. For True, it returned False and vice versa. For a *0*, it returned a True and for a non-zero number, it returned a False. In the other cases, each element is compared to other respective elements, that is, 1st element in x is compared to 1st element in y, 2nd element in x is compared to 2nd element in y, etc.

Assignment Operators

We use assignment operators to assign values to the variables. R supports the following assignment operators:

- <-, <<-, = :Leftwards assignment
- ->, ->> :Rightwards assignment

The = and <- operators can be used interchangeably to assign a variable a value in the same environment. The <<- operator should be used to assign values in parent environments similar to global assignments. The rightward assignments are not very commonly used even though they are available. The following example demonstrates how to use these operators:

```
x <- 4

x = 10

7 -> x
```

The above statements run as follows:

```
> x <- 4
> x
[1] 4
> x = 10
> x
[1] 10
> 7 -> x
> x
[1] 7
> |
```

Operator Precedence

When several operators are used in an expression, we need to know the order which the execution will be done. Some operators are given high precedence over others, meaning that they will be executed first regardless of their position in the expression.

Consider the following example:

```
1 + 5 * 3
```

The expression will run as shown below:

```
> 1 + 5 * 3
[1] 16
>|
```

The * operator was given a higher priority than the + operator, meaning that the expression was treated as *1 + (5 * 3)*. If you need to change the order of execution, you can enclose the parts in *parenthesis ()*. For example:

(1 + 5) * 3

This will run as follows:

```
> (1 + 5) * 3
[1] 18
>|
```

The expression placed within the parenthesis () was given the highest priority, hence, the result is not the same to what we got when not using parenthesis.

Operator Associativity

We are allowed to have more than one operators of similar precedence in the same expression. If that is the case, then the order of execution will be determined through associativity. Consider the example given below:

3 / 4 / 5

The expression will run as shown below:

```
> 3 / 4 / 5
[1] 0.15
>
```

The / has a left to right associativity. This means that the expression was evaluated as (3 / 4) / 5. If we need to change the order of execution, we can enclose the prioritized part within parenthesis. For example:

```
3 / (4 / 5)
```

This will run as shown below:

```
> 3 / (4 / 5)
[1] 3.75
>
```

The following table shows operator precedence and associativity in R. The operators have also been arranged according to decreasing order of precedence, that is, from highest to lowest:

Operator symbol	Associativity
^	Right to Left
-x, +x	Left to Right

%%	Left to Right
*, /	Left to Right
+, −	Left to Right
<, >, <=, >=, ==,	Left to Right
!	Left to Right
&, &&	Left to Right
|, ||	Left to Right
->, ->>	Left to Right
<-, <<-	Right to Left
=	Right to Left

- Operators help us perform arithmetic and logical operations.

- R supports different types of operators.

- Arithmetic operators are used for performing mathematical operations.

- Relational operators help us perform various comparison operations.

- Assignment operators help us assign values to variables.

- Operator precedence determines the operator that is given the highest precedence.

- Operator associativity determines how operations are done when more than one operator with the same precedence are found in expression.

5 DECISION MAKING IN R

In this section, we will discuss how to use the various decision-making statements in R.

Decision making is very important in any programming language. Decision making involves creating multiple conditions that are to be tested by the program, together with statements that will be executed when a condition is true, and optionally, the statements that are to be executed when the condition is false.

R supports different decision-making statements. Let us discuss them one-by-one:

"If" Statement

The *if* statement consists of a Boolean followed by one or more statements. The statement takes the syntax given below:

```
if(boolean_expression) {

    // statement(s) to be executed if the
Boolean expression evaluates to true.

}
```

If the specified condition is found to be true, the statements inside the curly brace will be executed. If the specified condition evaluates to a *"false"*, the statements immediately after the *if* statement will be executed. Consider the example given below:

```
y <- 12L
if(is.integer(y)) {
    print("Y is an Integer")
}
```

On execution, the program will give you the following output:

```
[1] "Y is an Integer"
```

The specified condition checks whether variable y is an integer or not. Since the variable is an integer, the condition evaluated to a true, hence, the statement below it was executed.

Here is another example showing how to use the *if* statement:

```
age <- 16
if(age < 18){
print("Your age is less than 18 years")
}
```

The code will return the following upon execution:

```
[1] "Your age is less than 18 years"
```

In the *if* expression, we are checking whether the value of variable age is less than 18. We had set the value of age to 16. Since the condition evaluates to a *true*, the statement below it was executed.

The bad thing about the *if* expression is that nothing is done when the condition is false. Let us change the value of age to 20:

```
age <- 20
if(age < 18){
print("Your age is less than 18 years")
}
```

Since the value of age is greater than 18, the condition will evaluate to a false. The code will return nothing. We need a way of specifying what should be done when the condition is false. This is what we will discuss next.

if...else statement

In the *if...else* statement, the *if* helps us set the condition and the statements to be executed when the condition is true. The *else* part helps us specify the statements that will be executed when the condition is false. This statement takes the following syntax:

```
if(boolean_expression) {
   // statement(s) to execute if the Boolean
expression evaluates to true.
} else {
```

```
// statement(s) to execute if the Boolean
expression evaluates to false.

}
```

If the condition evaluates to a true, the statements within the *if* block will be executed, while *if* the condition evaluates to a *false*, the statements within the *else* block will be executed. Let us use the example of checking the value of age:

```
age <- 20
if(age < 18){
print("Your age is less than 18 years")
} else {
print("Your age is above 18 years")
}
```

The code will return the following upon execution:

```
[1] "Your age is above 18 years"
```

The else part was executed since the condition is false. Here is another example:

```
y <- c("what","was","it")
if("it" %in% y) {
    print("it was found")
```

```
} else {
    print("it was not found")
}
```

The code will return the following upon execution:

```
[1] "it was found"
```

We have created a vector with strings. Three strings have been added to the vector, that is, *what*, *was* and *it*. In the if condition, we are checking whether the word it can be found in the vector. The statement below the *if* was executed since the condition is *true*.

Let us search for a word which is not in the vector, say me:

```
y <- c("what","was","it")
if("me" %in% y) {
    print("me was found")
} else {
    print("me was not found")
}
```

The code will return the following output upon execution:

```
[1] "me was not found"
```

The word *me* was not found in the vector, hence, the statement below the else part was executed.

"if...else" Ladder

Also known as the *if...else...if* statement, it is used when there are more than 2 alternatives to be executed. It starts with an *if* statement, followed by an optional *else...if...*else statement, making it good for testing a number of conditions. The ladder takes the syntax given below:

```
if(boolean_expression 1) {

    // to execute if the Boolean expression 1
is true.

} else if( boolean_expression 2) {

    // to execute if the boolean expression 2
is true.

} else if( boolean_expression 3) {

    // to execute if the boolean expression 3
is true.

} else {

    // to execute if none of the above
condition is true.

}
```

This is demonstrated in the code given below:

```
y <- c("what","was","it")
```

```
if("It" %in% y) {

    print("it was found on the first time")

} else if ("it" %in% y) {

    print("it was found on the second time")

} else {

    print("No it was found")

}
```

Execution of the above program will give the following output:

```
[1] "it was found on the second time"
```

The vector y has three strings, *what, was,* and *it.* The search is case sensitive. In the *if condition,* we are searching for *It,* not *it.* The condition will become *false.* In the *else if condition,* we are searching for *it.* This condition will be *true,* hence the statement below it will be executed. If the *if and else if conditions* evaluate to a *false,* the *else* part will be executed.

Here is another example:

```
y <- 0

if (y < 0) {

print("y is a Negative number")

} else if (y > 0) {

print("y is a Positive number")

} else
```

```
print("y is Zero")
```

The code will return the following output upon execution:

```
[1] "y is Zero"
```

Both the *if* and the *else if conditions* evaluated to *false*, hence, the *else* part was executed.

Switch Statement

The *switch statement* allows for a particular variable to be tested for equality against a list of values. Each value is referred to as a case, and the variable to be switched has to be checked for every case that exists.

The statement takes the syntax given below:

```
switch(expression, case1, case2, case3....)
```

Consider the example given below:

```
y <- switch(
    2,
    "john",
    "alice",
    "peter",
    "george"
)
```

```
print(y)
```

The program should give you the following output once executed:

```
[1] "alice"
```

In the above case, we are evaluating the number **2**, hence the item of the list was returned. The *switch statement* returns the item that corresponds to the numeric value that is under evaluation. If you specify a numeric value that is out of range, you will get a **NULL**. Let us demonstrate this:

```
y <- switch(
    5,
    "john",
    "alice",
    "peter",
    "george"
)
print(y)
```

The script will return the following:

```
NULL
```

The list has 4 elements, but we are checking for the 5th element. A NULL has been returned.

We can also use a string expression in the *switch()* function. In that case, the value of the item that is matched will be returned. Let us create an example:

```
switch("name", "name" = "John", "age" = 20,
"country" = "USA")
```

The code will run as follows:

```
> switch("name", "name" = "John", "age" = 20, "country" = "USA")
[1] "John"
>
```

We are evaluating using the *name* string. This has been matched to the first item and its value has been returned. Consider the next example given below:

```
switch("age", "name" = "John", "age" = 20,
"country" = "USA")
```

The code will run as follows:

```
> switch("age", "name" = "John", "age" = 20, "country" = "USA")
[1] 20
>
```

We have used the *age* as the string for evaluation. The second item has been matched; hence, its value has been returned.

- R supports a number of *decision-making* statements. These help us evaluate a condition or a set of conditions and take action based on the outcome of the evaluation.

- The *if statement* checks for the truth value of a condition and instruct the R interpreter on what to do when the condition is true.

- The *if...else statement* uses an if statement and an else part to specify the action to perform when the condition is false.

- The *if...else* ladder helps us evaluate multiple conditions and take different actions based on the outcome of each condition.

- The *switch statement* helps us check or evaluate the value of an item against a set of values.

6 R LOOPS

In this chapter, you will learn how to repeat the execution of certain parts of your R code using loops.

In some cases, you may be in need of executing a section of code for a number of times. Loops can help you achieve this effectively. Generally, loops execute the statements according to the order they have been written.

R supports different types of loop statements. Let us discuss them:

repeat Loop

With this loop, a piece of code will be executed again and again until it finds a *stop condition*. The repeat loop does not have a condition to check so as to exit the loop. We have to explicitly add the condition inside the loop body and use the *break statement* so as to exit the loop. If we don't do so, we will have created an infinite loop. The repeat loop in R takes the following syntax:

```
repeat {

   commands

   if(condition) {

      break

   }

}
```

Consider the example given below which shows how this loop can be used:

```
msg <- c("Hello","World!")
count <- 2
repeat {

   print(msg)

   count <- count+1

   if(count > 5) {

      break

   }

}
```

Write the script in an r script file and execute it from the terminal of your OS. it will return the following output:

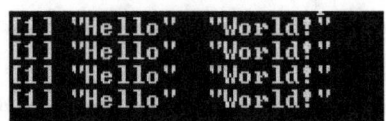

We have created two variables, *msg*, and *count*. The first one has a list of strings while the second variable holds the integer 2. Inside the body of the repeat loop, we are trying to print the value of *msg* variable. The counting will begin at number 2 because the value of variable count was initialized to 2. We have used the *if statement* to create a condition. The condition will ensure that the value of variable count does not go beyond 5. The loop will iterate from 2 to 5, meaning that the value of *msg variable* will be printed for only 4 times. That is how we got the above output! If it were not for the condition inside the *if statement*, the loop would run forever.

Here is another example:

```
y <- 1
repeat {
print(y)
y = y+1
if (y == 5){
break
}
}
```

The script will return the following upon execution:

We initialized the value of variable *y* to *1*. In the *if condition,* we are checking for when the value of this variable is *5,* at which the loop should stop. That is why the loop printed values only between *1* and *4,* with *4* included.

While Loop

This type of loop will execute code again and again until it meets a particular condition. The loop takes the syntax given below:

```
while (test_expression) {

    statement

}
```

The *test_expression* will be evaluated first before getting into the loop body. If the *test_expression* is true, the loop body will be executed. After execution of the loop body, execution will return to the *test_expression*. If true, the loop body will be executed again. With such a syntax, the loop might end up not running. If the *test_expression* is found to be false for the first time, the loop will have to be skipped, and then the statement that occurs immediately after the loop body will be executed. Consider the example given below:

```
msg <- c("Hello","this is a while loop")
count <- 2
while (count < 6) {
    print(msg)
    count = count + 1
```

```
}
```

The script should return the following result:

```
[1] "Hello"                    "this is a while loop"
[1] "Hello"                    "this is a while loop"
[1] "Hello"                    "this is a while loop"
[1] "Hello"                    "this is a while loop"
```

Here is another example that demonstrates the use of the *while* loop:

```
y <- 1
while (y < 6) {
print(y)
y = y+1
}
```

The script will return the following output upon execution:

```
[1] 1
[1] 2
[1] 3
[1] 4
[1] 5
```

The code returns numbers from 1 to 5.

for Loop

This is a repetition control structure that helps R programmers to write a loop that executes a particular section of code for a specific number of times. The statement takes the basic syntax given below:

```
for (value in vector) {
    statements
}
```

The *for* loop is very flexible since it is not limited to numbers or integers as the input. We can pass logical vectors, character vectors, and expressions or lists to it. Consider the example given below:

```
l <- LETTERS[1:5]
for ( j in l) {
    print(j)
}
```

Execution of the above program will return the following output:

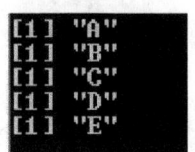

We have created a variable *l*. The LETTERS is an R keyword which represents all letters of the alphabet from A to Z, uppercase. The variable l will store the first 5 letters, that is, from A to E. We have then used a for loop to iterate through these. We have lastly printed them on the terminal.

Here is another example:

```
y <- c(3,5,2,9,7,11,4)
count <- 0
for (val in y) {
if(val %% 2 == 0)
count = count+1
}
print(count)
```

The script will return the following output upon execution:

We have created a vector *y* with a number of integers. The *variable count* has been initialized to 0. Inside the *for loop*, we have created the *variable val* to help us iterate the elements of the vector. We have used the *if statement* to check whether there are even numbers inside vector y. An integer is an even number if it gives a remainder of 0 after division by 2. The *count variable* helps us count the number of even numbers found inside the vector. From the output, only 2 even numbers were found.

Loop Control Statements

The purpose of loop control statements is to change the execution of a loop from its normal sequence. After execution has left a scope, all automatic objects that had been created within that scope will be destroyed. R supports two loop control statements, break and next. Let us discuss them:

break Statement

This *break statement* has two use cases in R:

- When the statement is found inside a loop, the loop is terminated immediately and the program control resumes in the next statement that follows outside the loop.

- We can use the *break statement* to terminate a case contained in a *switch statement*.

The statement takes the following syntax:

```
break
```

Consider the example given below:

```
msg <- c("Hello","World!")
count <- 2
repeat {
    print(msg)
    count <- count + 1
```

```
if(count > 6) {

    break

 }

}
```

Execution of the above program will return the following output:

```
[1] "Hello"   "World!"
[1] "Hello"   "World!"
[1] "Hello"   "World!"
[1] "Hello"   "World!"
[1] "Hello"   "World!"
```

We created two variables, *msg*, and *count*. The former stores a list of strings while the latter has been initialized to 2. Inside the repeat loop, we are printing the value of the *msg variable*. The value of the *counter variable* will be incremented by 1 after every iteration. We have then used the *if statement* to check for when the value of the *variable counter* is greater than 6. At this point, the loop should break or halt execution. The loop will execute for values of counter from 2 to 6. That is why the string was printed only 5 times.

Here is another example:

```
y <- 1:5

for (val in y) {

if (val == 4){

break
```

```
}

print(val)

}
```

The script will return the following output:

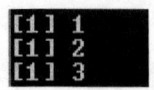

The variable y holds integers from 1 to 5. We have added a condition that makes the *for loop* break when the value of the iteration *variable val* is 4. That is why the script 1 to 3.

next Statement

The next statement helps us skip the current iteration of the loop and continue to the next iteration without terminate the execution of the loop. When the R interpreter encounters this statement in the program, it will skip any further evaluation and then start the next iteration of our loop. The statement takes the following syntax:

```
next
```

Consider the example shown below which shows how this statement can be used in R:

```
l <- LETTERS[1:6]
```

```
for ( j in l) {

    if (j == "C") {

        next

    }
    print(j)

}
```

Execution of the program should return the following output:

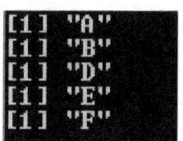

We have created the variable l to store the first 6 letters of the alphabet in uppercase. We have used the *if statement* inside the for loop to check for when the iteration variable j reaches C. At this point, the loop should skip to the next iteration. That is why the loop did not return C in the output.

Here is another example:

```
l <- 0:5

for (val in l) {

if (val == 2){

next

}
```

```
print(val)

}
```

The script will return the following output upon execution:

The variable *I* stores all integers from 0 to 5. We have then used the *if statement* for when the value of the iteration *variable val* is 2, at which point the loop should skip to the next iteration. That is why 2 is not part of the above output.

- Loops help us perform tasks repetitively.
- R supports different types of loop statements.
- The repeat loop can be used to run a section of code repeatedly until a certain condition is met.
- The while loop will execute a section of code until a certain condition is met.
- The for loop can be used to execute a loop for a specified number of times.
- R provides two loop control statements, break and next.
- The break statement helps us halt the execution of a loop when a specified condition is met.

- The next statement can be used to skip the execution of a certain loop iteration and skip to the next iteration.

7 R FUNCTIONS

In this chapter, you will learn how to create and use functions in R.

A function is simply a set of statements that have been put together for the purpose of performing a specific task. With functions, a code can be broken into simpler parts which are easy to understand and maintain. R comes with many in-built functions. It also allows its users to create their own functions.

In R, functions are treated as objects, meaning that the R interpreter is capable of passing control to the function, together with the arguments which may be good for the function to accomplish its tasks. The function will then perform its tasks and pass control to the interpreter and the results which might have been stored in the other functions.

Function Definition

To define a function in R, we use the function keyword. It takes the syntax given below:

```
function_name <- function(argument_1,
argument_2, ...) {

    Function body

}
```

The following are the different parts of the function:

1. *Function Name*- this is the actual name of the function. It is stored as an object with that name in the R environment.

2. *Arguments*- this is just a placeholder. Once the function has been invoked, a value will be passed to the argument. The arguments can have default values, but arguments are optional in a function since functions can be used without arguments.

3. *Function Body*- this is a collection of statements that define what the function will do.

4. *Return value*- this is the last expression in our function body which is to be evaluated.

R allows us to define our own functions. Each user-defined function is specific to what the user needs and we can use them just like the in-built functions. The example given below shows how to create and use a function in R:

```
# A function to return the squares of numbers
in a sequence.

new.function <- function(x) {
```

```
for(j in 1:x) {

    y <- j^2

    print(y)

}

}
```

We have defined a function named new. function that takes one argument x. The function will create a sequence from the value of this argument and get the square of each number in the sequence. For now, we have just defined the function without calling it, so when you run the code, you won't get any output. Here is another example:

```
pow <- function(a, b) {
# function to print a raised to the power b
result <- a^b
print(paste(a,"raised to power", b, "is",
result))
}
```

Above, we have defined a function named *pow*. The function takes two arguments, a and b. The function will then get the result of rising *a* to power of *b*. The result of this will be assigned to the variable named *result*.

Function Calls

We have mentioned a *function call*. A function call is done using the name of the function. If the function accepts arguments, then they should be passed during the function call.

Let us demonstrate how a function is called in R. We will use the function we created earlier, the new.function():

```
# A function to return the squares of numbers
in a sequence.
new.function <- function(x) {
    for(j in 1:x) {
        y <- j^2
        print(y)
    }
}
```

```
# Call the function new.function() and pass
the argument 5 as an argument.
new.function(5)
```

The program will return the following when executed:

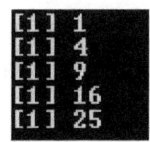

```
[1] 1
[1] 4
[1] 9
[1] 16
[1] 25
```

Also, it is possible for us to call a function without using an argument. The example given below best demonstrates this:

```
# A function to return the squares of numbers
in a sequence.

new.function <- function(x) {

    for(j in 1:5) {

        y <- j^2

        print(y)

    }

}
```

```
# Call the function new.function() and pass
no argument to it.

new.function()
```

Execution of the above program will return the following output:

When calling a function, we can specify the value of the arguments using either their names or position. This means that the arguments have to be supplied in the same order that they were defined in the function, or maybe supplied in a different sequence but assigned by use of their names. Consider the example given below:

```
# A function that takes 3 arguments.

new.function <- function(x, y, z) {

   result <- x * y + z

   print(result)

}

# Call the function by the position of
arguments.

new.function(4, 3, 12)

# Calling the function by the names of
arguments.

new.function(x = 10, y = 7, z = 2)
```

Execution of the above program will give the following output:

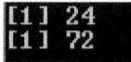

```
[1] 24
[1] 72
```

It is possible for us to have default arguments for a function. With such, we can call the function without passing arguments to it, and the default arguments will be used to provide the result. At the same time, we can pass in new values and this will allow us to get another result rather than the default one. Consider the example given below:

```
# Create a function with default arguments.

new.function <- function(x = 2, y = 6) {

   result <- x * y
```

```
    print(result)

}
```

```
# Call the function without passing arguments
to it.
```

```
new.function()
```

```
# Call the function and pass values for the
arguments
```

```
new.function(7,5)
```

Execution of the above program will return the following:

In the first call, we did not pass arguments to the function. The default values of the arguments were used to calculate the result. In the second call to the function, we passed new values to the arguments, 7 and 5. These were used to calculate the result.

Lazy Evaluation of a Function

The function arguments are usually evaluated lazily, meaning that they will only be executed when the function body needs them. Let us use an example to demonstrate this:

```
# Create a function that accepts arguments.
new.function <- function(x, y) {
    print(x^2)
```

```
print(x)

print(y)

}
```

```
# Evaluate the function by supplying only one
of the arguments.
```

```
new.function(8)
```

The script will return the following output upon execution:

```
[1] 64
[1] 8
Error in print(y) : argument "y" is missing, with no default
Calls: new.function -> print
Execution halted
```

The reason for the error is because the value of argument y was not provided during a call to the function, neither is there a default value assigned to the function.

return() Function

When creating functions, we will mostly want to have the function do some processing and return some result to us. In R, we can achieve using the *return() function*. The function takes the syntax given below:

```
return(expression)
```

The function can return any value which is a valid R object. Let us create an example that demonstrates how to use this function:

```r
checkFunc <- function(y) {
if (y > 0) {
result <- "y is Positive"
}
else if (y < 0) {
result <- "y is Negative"
}
else {
result <- "y is Zero"
}
return(result)
}
```

Let us perform sample runs by calling the *checkFunction() function* and pass some arguments to it:

```r
checkFunc(2)
checkFunc(-3)
checkFunc(0)
```

They will run as follows:

```
> checkFunc(2)
[1] "y is Positive"
> checkFunc(-3)
[1] "y is Negative"
> checkFunc(0)
[1] "y is Zero"
>
```

If we don't have explicit returns from any function, the value obtained from the last expression to be evaluated will be returned automatically. The following example demonstrates this:

```
checkFunc <- function(y) {
if (y > 0) {
result <- "y is Positive"
}
else if (y < 0) {
result <- "y is Negative"
}
else {
result <- "y is Zero"
}
result
}
```

Explicit *return() functions* should only be used when we need to return a value immediately from a function. If it's not the function's last statement, it will end the function prematurely and control will shift to the place where it was called.

The following example demonstrates this:

```
checkFunc <- function(y) {
if (y > 0) {
return("y is Positive")
}
else if (y < 0) {
return("y is Negative")
}
else {
return("y is Zero")
}
}
```

In the example given above, in case the $y > 0$, then the function will immediately return y is Positive without going further to evaluate the rest of the function body.

Multiple Returns

The *return() function* can return only a single object in R. If our goal is to return multiple values, we can create a list or any other object then return it. The following example demonstrates this:

```
multi_return <- function() {
```

```
employee <- list("name" = "john", "age" = 20,
"dept" = "ICT")

return(employee)

}
```

We have created a list named *employee* with many elements and we have returned the list. The function can be invoked as follows:

```
x <- multi_return()
```

We can then invoke the elements of the list using the variable x. This is shown below:

```
x$name

x$age

x$dept
```

These should execute as shown below:

```
> x <- multi_return()
> x$name
[1] "john"
> x$age
[1] 20
> x$dept
[1] "ICT"
>
```

Variable Scope

The scope of a variable determines the place within a program from which it can be accessed. The scope of a function is determined by the place of a declaration of the variable in relation to the function, that is, whether inside or outside the function. There are two types of variables based on scope in R:

- Global variables
- Local variables

Global Variables

A global variable is a type of a variable that will exist throughout the execution of a program. A global variable can be accessed and modified from any section of the program. However, a global variable will also depend on the perspective of a function.

Consider the example given below:

```
func_one <- function() {
b <- 1
func_two <- function() {
c <- 5
}
}
a <- 4
```

In our above example, we have two functions, *func_one()* and *func_two()*. We also have three variables, a, b and c with their values initialized. The variables a and b are global in relation to the function *function_two()*. This is because they have been declared outside the body of the function. From the perspective of *function_one()*, only variable a is global. This is because it has been declared outside the body of the function.

Local Variables

Although a global variable exists throughout the execution of the program, a local variable exists only within a particular part of a program such as a function and it will be released after the end of the function call. Let us use our previous example to demonstrate how a local variable works:

```
func_one <- function(){
b <- 1
func_two <- function(){
c <- 5
}
}
a <- 4
```

In the above example, variable c is a local variable. If a value is assigned to a variable using *function_two()*, this change will remain local and it won't be accessible from outside the function. This also occurs if a match occurs between the names of global and local variables. Consider the example given below:

```
func_one <- function(){
```

```
a <- 12
func_two <- function(){
a <- 20
print(a)
}
func_two()
print(a)
}
```

Let us call the functions and see what will happen:

```
x <- 9
func_one()
print(x)
```

These will run as follows:

```
> x <- 9
> func_one()
[1] 20
[1] 12
> x
[1] 9
>
```

The variable has been created locally within the environment frame of the two functions and it is different from the one of the global environment frames.

Accessing Global Variables

It is possible for us to access a global variable but the moment we try to assign a value to it, a new local variable will be created. To assign a value to a local variable, we should use the super assignment operator, that is, <<-.

When this operator is used within a function, it will search for the variable from the parent environment frame. If it's not found, it will continue to search in the next level until it has reached the global environment. If the variable is not found in the global environment, it will be created and assigned at the global level. Here is an example:

```r
func_one <- function(){
func_two <- function(){
a <<- 4
print(a)
}
func_two()
print(a)
}
```

Let us invoke the function named *func_one()*:

```r
func_one()
print(a)
```

These will run as follows:

```
> func_one()
[1] 4
[1] 4
> a
[1] 4
> |
```

When the R interpreter encountered the statement a <<- 4 within *func_two()*, it will have to look for the variable a in the *func_one()* *environment*. If this fails, the search will be continued in the R_GlobalEnv.

Since a has not been defined in the global environment, it will be created there and assigned. It will then be referenced and printed from there by both *func_one() and func_two()*.

Recursive Functions

A recursive function is a function that calls itself, and this process is known as recursion. It is a special programming technique that can be used in solving problems by breaking them into simpler and smaller sub-problems. We will create an example that makes this simple to understand.

We will create an example that calculates the factorial of a positive number. The factorial of a number is the product of all integers from 1 to the number. For example, the factorial of 4, written as 4! can be calculated as follows:

$$4! = 1*2*3*4 = 24$$

We can simplify this problem by creating a sub-problem as shown below:

```
4! = 4 * 3!
```

The sub-problem states that the factorial of 4 is 4 multiplied by the factorial of 3. This can be expressed using the following equation:

```
n! = n*(n-1)!
```

We can continue until we have reached 0!, which is 1. Let us create an example that demonstrates this:

```r
# A recursive function to calculate factorial
recursive.factorial <- function(a) {
if (a == 0)
return (1)
else
return (a * recursive.factorial(a-1))
}
```

We have created a function that will call itself. A statement like *recursive.factorial(a)* will become a * *recursive.factorial(a)* until when the value of a becomes equal to 0.

After a has become 0, the function will return 1 since the 0! is 1. This marks the terminating condition of our function, making it very important. Let us make some calls to the above function:

```
recursive.factorial(0)

recursive.factorial(8)

recursive.factorial(10)

recursive.factorial(7)
```

The above will run as follows:

```
> recursive.factorial(0)
[1] 1
> recursive.factorial(8)
[1] 40320
> recursive.factorial(10)
[1] 3628800
> recursive.factorial(7)
[1] 5040
>
```

When we use recursion, the code becomes shorter and simpler. However, recursive functions may sometimes be memory intensive as a result of nested function calls.

- A function puts related together. A function helps break a large program into small parts that are easy to understand and manage.
- To define a function R, we use the *function keyword*.

- A function may or may not take arguments. Default arguments can also be used in functions.

- When arguments are passed to the function during the function call, the default arguments are overridden.

- The scope of a variable determined the location from which it can be accessed within the program.

- A global variable is accessible from anywhere within the program, and it is available throughout the program execution period.

- A local variable can only be accessed from within a function. It is only available during the lifetime of the function.

- A recursive function is a function that calls itself repeatedly.

8 R CLASSES AND OBJECTS

In this chapter, you will learn the various object-oriented programming features supported by R.

R supports the features of object-oriented programming. Actually, R treats everything as an object.

An R object refers to a data structure with attributes and methods that act on the attributes.

A *class* is a blueprint of an object. Think of a class as a sketch/prototype of a house. It describes the details of windows, floor, doors, etc. The house will then be build based on the description.

The house is the object. This is because we can build many houses from the description, meaning that it is also possible for us to create many objects from a class. An object is also referred to as an instance of a class and the process of creating an object from a class is referred to as instantiation.

Most programming languages have a single class system, but R comes with 3 different class systems. These include the following:

- S3 class
- S4 class
- Reference class

Each class system has its own features and peculiarities, and the choosing of one over the other is simply a matter of preference. Let us discuss each of them:

S3 Class

This type of R class system is primitive in nature. It doesn't have a formal definition. To create an object of this class, we simply have to add a class attribute to it. Such simplicity explains why this class is highly used in R programming. Actually, majority of the in-built classes are of this type. Let us create an example that demonstrates this:

Defining S3 Classes

There is no formal or predefined way to defining an S3 class. A list whose class attribute has been set to a class name is an S3 object. The list components will become the member variables of the object.

We will create a list that has all the required components. A class will then be created from that list.

```
s <- list(name = "Alice", age = 20, GPA = 3.5)
```

We can now name the class:

```
class(s) <- "student"
```

The two commands should run as shown below:

```
> s <- list(name = "Alice", age = 20, GPA = 3.5)
> class(s) <- "student"
>
```

We have created a class from the list and the class has been given the name *student*. We have gone further to create an object from the class, and the object has been named *s*. To see the details of this object, just type its name on the R console and hit the return key as shown below:

```
> s
$name
[1] "Alice"

$age
[1] 20

$GPA
[1] 3.5

attr(,"class")
[1] "student"
>
```

If you are used to programming languages such as Python and C++ that come with formal class and object definitions, this may seem to be awkward to you. Such languages also have properly defined attributes and methods for classes.

R allows you to convert an object's class depending on your requirements with an object of the same class that looks completely different.

Creating Objects from Constructors

Many are the cases we use a function having the same name as a class to create objects. Such a mechanism brings uniformity when it comes to the creation of objects and it makes them look the same.

It is possible for us to impose integrity checks when it comes to the attributes. The class attributes of an object can be set using the *attr() function*. Let us demonstrate this by creating a constructor of the student class:

```r
# create a list

s <- list(name = "Alice", age = 20, GPA = 3.5)

# create a class

class(s) <- "student"

# create a constructor function for class "student"

student <- function(n,a,g) {

# impose integrity checks

if(g>4 || g<0)  stop("Student's GPA must be between 0 and 4")

value <- list(name = n, age = a, GPA = g)

# we can set a class using either the class() or attr() function

attr(value, "class") <- "student"
```

```
value

}
```

We can now use the constructor to create objects:

```
s <- student("John", 24, 3.7)
```

The above will run as follows:

```
> s <- student("John", 24, 3.7)
> s
$name
[1] "John"

$age
[1] 24

$GPA
[1] 3.7

attr(,"class")
[1] "student"
>
```

Remember that we imposed a constraint that the GPA must range between 0 and 4. Let us create an object which violates this constraint and see what will happen:

```
s <- student("Alice", 22, 5)
```

In the above example, the GPA is 5, meaning that it violates the constraint. The script will run as shown below:

```
> s <- student("Alice", 22, 5)
Error in student("Alice", 22, 5) : Student's GPA must be between 0 and 4
>
```

An error has been generated because the constraint has been violated. Note that the constraint will only be applied when we create an object using the constructor.

Methods and Generic Functions

Anytime we write the name of the object, all its internals will be printed. While in the interactive mode, anytime we type the name, it will be printed by use of the *print() function*. This is shown below:

```
> s
$name
[1] "John"

$age
[1] 24

$GPA
[1] 3.7

attr(,"class")
[1] "student"
>
```

The *print()* *method* can also be used with matrices, vectors, factors, data frames, etc. and they will be printed differently based on the class to which they belong.

The question is, how does the *print() function* know how to print such different objects? The answer to this question is that *print()* is a generic function. The function has a collection of various methods. You can look for such methods by running the following script:

```
methods(print)
```

The script will run as follows:

```
> methods(print)
  [1] print.acf*
  [2] print.all_vars*
  [3] print.anova*
  [4] print.any_vars*
  [5] print.aov*
  [6] print.aovlist*
  [7] print.ar*
  [8] print.Arima*
  [9] print.arima0*
 [10] print.AsIs
 [11] print.aspell*
 [12] print.aspell_inspect_context*
 [13] print.bibentry*
 [14] print.Bibtex*
 [15] print.BoolResult*
```

From the above list, you can see methods such as *print.factor* and *print.data.fra*me. This means that when you call the *print()* on a factor, the call will be dispatched to the *print.factor()*. The method names are in the form of *generic_name.class_name()*. That is how knows the method to call based on the class.

When we print the object of student class, it will look for a method of the form *print.student()*, but no method of such a form will be found.

The object of the class student called the method *print.default()*. This is simply the fallback method that will be called if no match is found. Generic functions come with default methods. R comes with many generic functions like *print()*. To see them, we need to run the following script:

```
methods(class="default")
```

The script will run as shown below:

```
> methods(class="default")
 [1] add1            aggregate        AIC            all.equal
 [5] ansari.test     anyDuplicated    aperm          ar.burg
 [9] ar.yw           as.array         as.character   as.data.frame
[13] as.Date         as.dist          as.expression  as.function
[17] as.hclust       as.list          as.matrix      as.null
[21] as.person       as.personList    as.POSIXct     as.POSIXlt
[25] as.single       as.stepfun       as.table       as.ts
[29] Axis            barplot          bartlett.test  BIC
[33] biplot          boxplot          by             case.names
[37] cdplot          chol             coef           confint
[41] contour         cophenetic       cor.test       cut
[45] cycle           deltat           density        deriv
```

Creating Own Methods

It is possible for us to implement the *print.student()* method. Let us demonstrate this:

```
print.student <- function(obj) {
cat(obj$name, "\n")
cat(obj$age, "years old\n")
cat("GPA:", obj$GPA, "\n")
}
```

The above method will be called anytime that we need to print an object of the *student class*. In the S3 class system, methods, don't belong to any class or object, but they belong to the *generic function*s. This works provided the class of the object has been set. Let us demonstrate this:

```
> s
John
24 years old
GPA: 3.7
>
```

The method implemented above has been called. Let us remove the class attribute:

```
unclass(s)
```

This will run as follows:

```
> unclass(s)
$name
[1] "John"

$age
[1] 24

$GPA
[1] 3.7

>
```

Creating Generic Functions

R allows us to create our own generic functions such as *print()* and *plot()*. To see the implementation of these functions, just type them on the R console as shown below:

```
> print
function (x, ...)
UseMethod("print")
<bytecode: 0x08361020>
<environment: namespace:base>
> plot
function (x, y, ...)
UseMethod("plot")
<bytecode: 0x08522428>
<environment: namespace:graphics>
>
```

It is clear that each function has a single call to the *UseMethod()* and the name of the generic function has been passed to it. This makes the dispatcher function that handles all the background details. That is how simple it is for one to implement a generic function.

To demonstrate this, we will create a new generic function and give it the name *student.grade*.

```
student.grade <- function(obj) {
UseMethod("student.grade")

}
```

If a generic function has no method, it is useless. Let us add the default method to it:

```
student.grade.default <- function(obj) {
cat("A generic function\n")

}
```

We can now create a method for the *student* class:

```
student.grade.student <- function(obj) {
cat("Your grade is", obj$GPA, "\n")

}
```

All the above scripts should run successfully on the R console as shown below:

```
> student.grade <- function(obj) {
+ UseMethod("grade")
+ }
>
> student.grade <- function(obj) {
+ UseMethod("student.grade")
+ }
>
> student.grade.default <- function(obj) {
+ cat("A generic function\n")
+ }
>
> student.grade.student <- function(obj) {
+ cat("Your grade is", obj$GPA, "\n")
+ }
>
```

Here is a sample run that shows how the function will execute:

```
student.grade(s)
```

It should run as follows:

```
> student.grade(s)
Your grade is 3.7
> |
```

We have successfully implemented a generic function named *student.grade* and then a method for the class.

S4 Class

These types of classes are advanced compared to the S3 classes. They come with a formally defined structure that helps them make objects of the same class look similar. Its defined and a uniform way of creating objects makes code very safe and prevent us from making basic mistakes.

Defining S4 Classes

To define an S4 class, we use the *setClass() function*. In R, the member variables are referred to as slots. During a class definition, we are required to set the class name and the slots that it will have. The following example demonstrates how to define an S4 class in R:

```
setClass("student",
slots=list(name="character", age="numeric",
GPA="numeric"))
```

In the above example, we have created a class named *student* with three slots, *name, age,* and *GPA.*

Creating S4 Objects

To create objects from S4 classes, we use the *new() function*. Let us use an example to demonstrate this:

We will use the *new() function* to create an object. We will also provide the name of the class as well as the slots.

```
s <- new("student",name="Alice", age=20,
GPA=3.5)
```

You can view the details of the object by typing its name on the R console. The commands should run as shown below:

```
> setClass("student", slots=list(name="character", age="numeric", GPA="numeric"))
> s <- new("student",name="Alice", age=20, GPA=3.5)
> s
An object of class "student"
Slot "name":
[1] "Alice"

Slot "age":
[1] 20

Slot "GPA":
[1] 3.5

> |
```

To know whether an object is an S4 object, we can call the *isS4()* *function* then pass the name of the object to the function. The result will be either *TRUE* or *FALSE*. This is shown below:

```
isS4(s)
```

The above should run as shown below:

```
> isS4(s)
[1] TRUE
>
```

The above shows that s is an S4 object.

The *setClass() function* will return a generator function. The generator function usually has the same name as the class, and we can use it to create new objects. It acts in the same way as a constructor. This is demonstrated below:

```
student <- setClass("student",
slots=list(name="character", age="numeric",
GPA="numeric"))
```

We can then view the details of the class:

```
> student <- setClass("student", slots=list(name="character", age="numeric", GPA="numeric"))
> student
class generator function for class "student" from package '.GlobalEnv'
function (...)
new("student", ...)
> |
```

We can now use the above constructor function to create new objects. In the above example, the constructor uses the *new() function* to create new functions. See it as a wrap around. Let us now use the *generator function* to create an *S4 object*.

```
student(name="George", age=22, GPA=3.0)
```

The script will run as shown below:

```
> student(name="George", age=22, GPA=3.0)
An object of class "student"
Slot "name":
[1] "George"

Slot "age":
[1] 22

Slot "GPA":
[1] 3

> |
```

Modifying Slots

R allows us to access and modify the slots. To access the components of a list, we used the $, but to access a slot of an object, we use the @. Here is how we can access the slots:

```
s@name

s@age

s@GPA
```

They should run as shown below:

```
> s@name
[1] "Alice"
> s@age
[1] 20
> s@GPA
[1] 3.5
>
```

We can modify a slot through reassignment. This is shown below:

Let us modify the GPA:

```
s@GPA <- 3.6
```

```
> s@GPA <- 3.6
> s
An object of class "student"
Slot "name":
[1] "Alice"

Slot "age":
[1] 20

Slot "GPA":
[1] 3.6

>
```

The output shows that the GPA has been modified successfully.

The slots can also be modified by use of the *slot() function*. Let us demonstrate this:

```
slot(s,"name")
slot(s,"name") <- "Antony"
```

The scripts will run as follows:

```
> slot(s,"name")
[1] "Alice"
> slot(s,"name") <- "Antony"
> s
An object of class "student"
Slot "name":
[1] "Antony"

Slot "age":
[1] 20

Slot "GPA":
[1] 3.6

> |
```

The output shows that the name was changed from Alice to Antony.

Methods and Generic Functions

Just like the S3 class, S4 class methods also belong to the *generic functions* instead of the class itself. The S4 generics can be used in much the same way as the S3 generics.

We can use the *showMethods() function* to list all the S4 generic functions and methods.

```
showMethods()
```

When the name of the object is written in the interactive mode, it will be printed.

We use the *show() function*, which is an S4 generic function. Let us use the *isS4() function* to check whether a function is generic or not:

```
isS4(show)
isS4(print)
```

These will run as follows:

```
> isS4(show)
[1] TRUE
> isS4(print)
[1] FALSE
>
```

Writing Own Methods

To create our own method, we can use the *setMethod()* helper function. Here is an example showing how we can implement the class method for *show() generic*:

```
setMethod("show",
"student",
function(object) {
cat(object@name, "\n")
cat(object@age, "years old\n")
cat("GPA:", object@GPA, "\n")
}
```

)

```
> setMethod("show",
+ "student",
+ function(object) {
+ cat(object@name,  "\n")
+ cat(object@age, "years old\n")
+ cat("GPA:", object@GPA, "\n")
+ }
+ )
>
```

Now, if the name of the object is written in the interactive mode, the script given above will be executed. Let us see this in action:

```
s <- new("student",name="Cate", age=21,
GPA=3.4)
```

It should run as follows:

```
> s <- new("student",name="Cate", age=21, GPA=3.4)
> s
Cate
21 years old
GPA: 3.4
>
```

Reference Class

The reference class system is similar to the object-oriented programming we use in other programing languages such as Java and

C++. It was introduced later. The reference class is simply S4 class with an environment added to it.

Defining Reference Classes

A reference class can be defined in the same way as an S4 class. However, instead of using the *setClass() function,* we use the *setRefClass() function.* The name of the class is passed as the argument to the function. Let us demonstrate this:

```
setRefClass("student")
```

The member variables for the class should be part of the definition. In the reference class system, the member variables are referred to as fields. Here is how we can define a reference class in R with three fields:

```
setRefClass("student", fields = list(name =
"character", age = "numeric", GPA =
"numeric"))
```

```
> setRefClass("student", fields = list(name = "character", age = "numeric", GPA = "numeric"))
>
```

Creating Reference Objects

The *setRefClass() function* gives us a generator function that can help us create objects of that class. This is demonstrated below:

```
student <- setRefClass("student", fields =
list(name = "character", age = "numeric", GPA
= "numeric"))
```

We now have a generator function named *student()*. We can use it to create new objects:

```
s <- student(name = "Alice", age = 20, GPA =
3.6)
```

The scripts should run as follows:

```
> student <- setRefClass("student", fields = list(name = "character", age = "numeric", GPA = "numeric"))
>
> s <- student(name = "Alice", age = 20, GPA = 3.6)
> s
Reference class object of class "student"
Field "name":
[1] "Alice"
Field "age":
[1] 20
Field "GPA":
[1] 3.6
>
```

Modifying Fields

For us to modify the fields, we must first access them. We can access the fields of an object using the $ operator. Here is an example:

s$name

s$age

s$GPA

These should run as follows:

```
> s$name
[1] "Alice"
> s$age
[1] 20
> s$GPA
[1] 3.6
>
```

To modify any field, we only have to reassign it. Let us change the name of the student:

```
s$name <- "Cate"
```

We can then view the details of the object to see whether the change was successful:

```
> s$name <- "Cate"
> s
Reference class object of class "student"
Field "name":
[1] "Cate"
Field "age":
[1] 20
Field "GPA":
[1] 3.6
>
```

Reference Methods

Methods that have been defined for a reference class do not belong to the generic functions as it is the case in S3 and S4 classes. All reference classes come with predefined methods since they are inherited from the envRefClass superclass.

```
> student
Generator for class "student":

Class fields:

Name:      name      age      GPA
Class: character   numeric   numeric

Class Methods:
    "field", "trace", "getRefClass", "initFields", "copy", "callSuper", ".objectPackage", "export",
    "untrace", "getClass", "show", "usingMethods", ".objectParent", "import"

Reference Superclasses:
    "envRefClass"

>
```

The above list shows methods such as *list()*, *copy()*, *field()* etc. It is possible for us to create our own methods for the class. To do this, we pass a list of function definitions to the methods argument of the *setRefClass() function* during class definition. Here is an example:

```
student <- setRefClass("student",

fields = list(name = "character", age =
"numeric", GPA = "numeric"),

methods = list(

increase_age = function(a) {

age <<- age + a

},

decrease_age = function(a) {

age <<- age - a

}

)
```

)

In the above code, we have defined two methods, *increase_age()* and *decrease_age()*, that will modify the age field.

We should use the non-local assignment operator, that is, <<-, since age is not in the local environment of the method. If we had used the simple assignment operator, that is, <-, a local variable named age would have been created. This is not what we need to achieve. In such a case, R will give us a warning.

The example given below demonstrates how to use the methods defined above:

First, let us create a new object:

```
s <- student(name = "Peter", age = 21, GPA = 
3.3)
```

Let us now use the methods. First, let us increase the age by 4 years:

```
s$increase_age(4)
s$age
```

```
> s <- student(name = "Peter", age = 21, GPA = 3.3)
> s$increase_age(4)
> s$age
[1] 25
```

The value of age has changed from 21 to 25. The *increase_age()* method worked successfully.

Let us now decrease the age by 5 years:

```
s$decrease_age(5)
s$age
```

```
> s$decrease_age(5)
> s$age
[1] 20
>
```

The value of age has changed from 25 to 20. The *decrease_age()* *method* worked successfully.

- R supports the features of object oriented programming. It treats everything as an object.
- A class is a blueprint or a template from which an object is created.
- An object is a data structure with attributes and methods for acting on those attributes.
- R supports three different types of classes, S3, S4, and Reference classes.
- The S3 class is a primitive class with no formal definition. To create an object in this class, we only have to assign a class attribute to it.
- The S4 classes are a bit advanced compared to S3 classes, and they come with a defined way of creating objects.

- The reference class is the most advanced in R, providing classes that are similar to the classes used in other object-oriented programming languages like Java and C++.

9 R FOR DATA SCIENCE

In this chapter, we will explore the basics of R for data science.

R is a great programming language used for statistical computing and data analysis. Since its initial launch in the early 1990s, a lot of efforts have been made to help improve its interface. It started as a basic text editor to interactive R Studio and then to jupyter notebooks and these have engaged many data scientists from all over the world.

R has benefitted a lot from its generously contributing users from all over the world. Its many packages have also made it more powerful and liked by data analysts. Its packages such as *dplyr, tidyr, readr, data. table, SparkR, ggplot2,* and others have made it easy for anyone to do data manipulation, computation and visualization much faster.

CSV Data

Loading Data

Before you can begin to analyze your data in R, you need to first analyze it. Your data can be stored in different file formats, including Excel, CSV, JSON, text, etc. R provides mechanisms for loading data stored in different formats.

Let us discuss how to load data kept in a .csv file. A CSV (comma separated values) file has items separated by commas. We will use the file *employees.csv* with the following data:

```
id,surname,wage,start_date,dept
1,John,656.3,2014-03-02,Finance
2,Mercy,498.2,2015-08-21,Operations
3,Kogan,711,2014-11-15,ICT
4,Milly,729,2016-05-12,HR
5,Gary,856.21,2015-03-22,Finance
6,Pendo,578,2014-06-21,ICT
7,Michael,488.8,2014-07-28,Operations
8,Gerald,622.5,2013-06-16,HR
```

The columns at the top are also separated with commas.

First, let us change the working directory to the location of the .csv file. Mine is kept in the admin directory. You can see the current directory that R is pointing at by running the following command:

```
getwd()
```

```
> getwd()
[1] "C:/Users/admin/Documents"
```

I need to change to the admin directory. I run the following command:

```
setwd("C:/Users/admin/")
```

We can then check the current directory that R is pointing at:

```
getwd()
```

```
> setwd("C:/Users/admin/")
> getwd()
[1] "C:/Users/admin"
>
```

To read csv data in R, we call the *read.csv()* *method*. Let us demonstrate this:

```
data <- read.csv("employees.csv")
print(data)
```

The code will return the following:

```
> data <- read.csv("employees.csv")
> print(data)
  id surname   wage start_date       dept
1  1    John 656.30 2014-03-02    Finance
2  2   Mercy 498.20 2015-08-21 Operations
3  3   Kogan 711.00 2014-11-15        ICT
4  4   Milly 729.00 2016-05-12         HR
5  5    Gary 856.21 2015-03-22    Finance
6  6   Pendo 578.00 2014-06-21        ICT
7  7 Michael 488.80 2014-07-28 Operations
8  8  Gerald 622.50 2013-06-16         HR
>
```

Analyzing the Data

By default, the *read.csv() function* loads your data into a data frame. It is possible for us to check this by running the following command:

```
print(is.data.frame(data))
```

```
> print(is.data.frame(data))
[1] TRUE
>
```

The return was a TRUE, showing that the data was loaded into a data frame.

We can also check the number of columns and rows contained in the data by calling the *ncol()* and *nrow() function* respectively. This is demonstrated below:

```
print(ncol(data))
print(nrow(data))
```

The code will run as follows:

```
> print(ncol(data))
[1] 5
> print(nrow(data))
[1] 8
>
```

The output shows that the data has 5 columns and 8 rows.

Now that we have our data in a data frame, we can apply all the functions that are applicable to a data frame.

We have a column named wage. We need to get the maximum wage. We simply have to run the following script:

```
wage <- max(data$wage)
print(wage)
```

The code will run as follows:

```
> wage <- max(data$wage)
> print(wage)
[1] 856.21
>
```

It is possible for us to run a command that filters the data in the same way we do in SQL. A good example is when we need to get the details of the employee who is paid the highest wage. We can run the following script for this:

```
wage <- max(data$wage)
det <- subset(data, wage == max(wage))
print(det)
```

The code will return the following:

```
> wage <- max(data$wage)
> det <- subset(data, wage == max(wage))
> print(det)
  id surname   wage start_date    dept
5  5    Gary 856.21 2015-03-22 Finance
>
```

Let us retrieve all employees who work in the Finance department:

```
data <- read.csv("employees.csv")
```

```
det <- subset( data, dept == "Finance")
print(det)
```

The code will return the following:

```
> det <- subset( data, dept == "Finance")
> print(det)
  id surname   wage start_date    dept
1  1    John 656.30 2014-03-02 Finance
5  5    Gary 856.21 2015-03-22 Finance
>
```

Let us get the details of the person who works in the ICT departments and earns more than 700:

```
data <- read.csv("employees.csv")

det <- subset(data, wage > 700 & dept ==
"ICT")

print(det)
```

The code will run as follows:

```
> data <- read.csv("employees.csv")
>
> det <- subset(data, wage > 700 & dept == "ICT")
> print(det)
  id surname wage start_date dept
3  3   Kogan  711 2014-11-15  ICT
>
```

We can also get the details of employees who joined the company from 2015:

```
data <- read.csv("employees.csv")
```

```
det <- subset(data, as.Date(start_date) >
as.Date("2015-01-01"))

print(det)
```

The code will run as follows:

```
> data <- read.csv("employees.csv")
>
> det <- subset(data, as.Date(start_date) > as.Date("2015-01-01"))
> print(det)
  id surname   wage start_date       dept
2  2   Mercy 498.20 2015-08-21 Operations
4  4   Milly 729.00 2016-05-12         HR
5  5    Gary 856.21 2015-03-22    Finance
>
```

Writing to the File

It is possible for us to create a csv file from a data frame in R. The csv file can be created using the *write.csv() function*. The file will be created in the current working directory. This is demonstrated below:

```
# First, we create the data frame.

data <- read.csv("employees.csv")

det <- subset(data, as.Date(start_date) >
as.Date("2015-01-01"))

# Write the filtered data into a new csv
file.

write.csv(det,"newfile.csv")

newdata <- read.csv("newfile.csv")
```

```
print(newdata)
```

The script should run successfully as shown below:

```
> # First, we create the data frame.
> data <- read.csv("employees.csv")
> det <- subset(data, as.Date(start_date) > as.Date("2015-01-01"))
>
> # Write the filtered data into a new csv file.
> write.csv(det,"newfile.csv")
> newdata <- read.csv("newfile.csv")
> print(newdata)
  X id surname  wage start_date       dept
1 2  2   Mercy 498.20 2015-08-21 Operations
2 4  4   Milly 729.00 2016-05-12         HR
3 5  5    Gary 856.21 2015-03-22    Finance
>
```

We first create a data frame from the file *employees.csv*. We have not simply loaded data from the file, but the data has been filled to be comprised of the details of only the employees who joined the company in 2015 and later. We have then created a new file, newfile.csv and loaded the data into it. We have then read the contents of this file and printed them on the R console.

We can see that there is a column X which is not useful. Let us drop the column:

```
data <- read.csv("employees.csv")

det <- subset(data, as.Date(start_date) >
as.Date("2015-01-01"))

# Write the filtered data into a new file.

write.csv(det,"newfile.csv", row.names =
FALSE)

newdata <- read.csv("newfile.csv")
```

```
print(newdata)
```

The code will run as follows:

```
> data <- read.csv("employees.csv")
> det <- subset(data, as.Date(start_date) > as.Date("2015-01-01"))
>
> # Write the filtered data into a new file.
> write.csv(det,"newfile.csv", row.names = FALSE)
> newdata <- read.csv("newfile.csv")
> print(newdata)
  id surname   wage start_date        dept
1  2   Mercy 498.20 2015-08-21  Operations
2  4   Milly 729.00 2016-05-12          HR
3  5    Gary 856.21 2015-03-22     Finance
>
```

The column X is now not shown. We have used the *row.names=FALSE* property to remove it. Note that this parameter should be used when writing to the file as shown above.

Excel Data

Microsoft Excel is the most widely used spread today. It stores data in .xls or .xlsx format. R has specific packages that can help us read data from such files. Examples of such packages include XLConnect, xlsx, gdata and others. We will use the xlsx package in this section. The package is dependent on other packages, hence, you may be asked to install them. The same package can also be used to write data into an Excel file.

Installing the Package

The first step should be for us to install the package. You just have to run the following command on the R console:

```
install.packages("xlsx")
```

You may be asked to install other packages on which the package depends. Just run the same command to install them.

It will be good for us to verify whether the package has been installed or not. We just need to run the following command:

```
any(grepl("xlsx",installed.packages()))
```

In my case, the command runs as follows:

```
> any(grepl("xlsx",installed.packages()))
[1] TRUE
>
```

It has returned a TRUE, meaning that the package is already installed.

Now that the library has been installed, we should load it into the R workspace and begin to use it. Here is the command for this:

```
library("xlsx")
```

The above command will load the library into the workspace.

Loading the Data

We can now load the data. We will use the file named *workers.xlsx*. To read data from this file, we can use the *read.xlsx()*.

The data will then be read into a data frame. Let us read the first worksheet from the *workers.xlsx file*:

```
data <- read.xlsx("workers.xlsx", sheetIndex
= 1)

print(data)
```

The code will run as follows:

```
> setwd("C:/Users/admin/")
> library("xlsx")
> setwd("C:/Users/admin/")
> data <- read.xlsx("workers.xlsx", sheetIndex = 1)
> print(data)
   ID   Name Age Retire
1   1 Daniel  55   2023
2   2  Joyce  45   2033
3   3 Joseph  55   2023
4   4 Joseph  35   2043
5   5   Lucy  42   2036
6   6 George  50   2028
7   7  James  30   2048
8   8  Agnes  24   2054
9   9  Bosco  33   2045
10 10 Jayden  35   2043
>
```

Now that we have the data, we can perform operations on it as we did in the previous case with *csv data*.

Statistical Analysis

R comes with many in-built functions that can be used for performing statistical analysis. Most of these functions are implemented in the R base package. The functions take in an R vector as the input together with other arguments and return the result. We will discuss three functions that can be used for statistical analysis in R, the mean, mode, and the median.

Mean

To calculate the mean of a dataset, the sum of all values is obtained and then divided by the total number of the values in the dataset. R provides the *mean() function* that can be used for calculating the mean of a dataset. Here is the syntax for calculating the mean of a dataset:

```
mean(x, trim = 0, na.rm = FALSE, ...)
```

In the above syntax, x denotes the input vector, trim will drop some of the observations from the ends of the sorted vector while *na.rm* will remove the missing values from the input vector. Consider the example given below:

```
x <- c(10, 7, 3, 52, 12, 4, 54, -21, 8, -7)
# Find the Mean.
result.mean <- mean(x)
print(result.mean)
```

The script will run as follows:

```
> x <- c(10, 7, 3, 52, 12, 4, 54, -21, 8, -7)
>
> # Find the Mean.
> result.mean <- mean(x)
> print(result.mean)
[1] 12.2
>
```

We began by creating a vector x with a set of 10 numerical values. We have then invoked *the mean() function* and passed the name of the vector to it as the argument and assigned the value obtained from the calculation to the variable *result.mean*. We have then printed the value of this variable.

When we use the trim option in the *mean() function*, the value will first be sorted and then the needed number of observations will be dropped from calculating the mean. Let us modify the previous example to demonstrate this:

```
x <- c(10, 7, 3, 52, 12, 4, 54, -21, 8, -7)
# Find the Mean.
result.mean <- mean(x, trim = 0.3)
print(result.mean)
```

In this case, when the vector elements are sorted, we will get the following:

```
-21, -7, 3, 4, 7, 8, 10, 12, 52, 54
```

Since we have set the trim to 0.3, 3 values will be trimmed from each end. This means that the values that will be removed and used for calculation of the mean will be -21, -7, 3 from the left and 12, 52, 54 from the right.

If missing values are found, the *mean()* will return NA. To do away with the missing values in the calculation, we should use the parameter *na.rm* = *TRUE*. This parameter simply means that NA values should be removed. Here is an example that demonstrates this:

```
x <- c(10, 7, 3, 52, 12, 4, 54, -21, 8, -7,
NA)
# Find the mean.
result.mean <-  mean(x)
print(result.mean)
# Calculate the mean while dropping the NA
values.
result.mean <-  mean(x,na.rm = TRUE)
print(result.mean)
```

The code will run as follows:

```
> x <- c(10, 7, 3, 52, 12, 4, 54, -21, 8, -7, NA)
>
> # Find the mean.
> result.mean <-  mean(x)
> print(result.mean)
[1] NA
>
> # Calculate the mean while dropping the NA values.
> result.mean <-  mean(x,na.rm = TRUE)
> print(result.mean)
[1] 12.2
>
```

We have created a vector whose elements include an NA. In the first instance of calculating the mean, the NA value has not been dropped, but it has been considered in the calculation. That is why an NA has first been returned. In the second instance of calculation of the mean, the NA value has been dropped before the calculation, hence, the calculation ran successfully.

Median

The median is the middle most item in a data set. In R, we use the *median() function* to calculate the median of a data set. The function is used with the following syntax:

```
median(x, na.rm = FALSE)
```

The x in the above syntax denotes the input vector while the *na.rm property* will be used to remove any missing values from the vector. Here is an example:

```
x <- c(10, 7, 3, 52, 12, 4, 54, -21, 8, -7)
# Calculate the median.
median.result <- median(x)
print(median.result)
```

```
> x <- c(10, 7, 3, 52, 12, 4, 54, -21, 8, -7)
> # Calculate the median.
> median.result <- median(x)
> print(median.result)
[1] 7.5
>
```

We began by creating a vector of 10 integers and given it the name x. We have then called the *median() function* and passed the name of the vector to it as the argument. The result of this operation has been assigned to the median. result variable. We have then printed the value of this variable, returning 7.5. This is the median of the data.

Mode

The mode refers to the item that occurs the highest number of times in a dataset. The mode of a dataset can have a numeric or character data, which is not the case with mean and median.

R does not provide us with an in-built function for calculating the mode of a dataset. This means that it is up to us to create our function that we can use to calculate the mode of our dataset. We will create such a function. The function will take a vector as an input and return the mode as the output:

```r
getmode <- function(y) {

    uniqvec <- unique(y)

    uniqvec[which.max(tabulate(match(y,
uniqvec)))]

}
# Create a vector of numbers.
y <- c(3, 1, 2, 2, 1, 2, 4, 4, 1, 5, 5, 1, 2,
1)
# Calculate the mode using the user function.
result <- getmode(y)
print(result)
# Create a vector of characters.
charvec <- c("i","was","the","was","it")
# Use the user function to calculate the mode
result <- getmode(charvec)
print(result)
```

First, we have created the *function getmode()* which will help us to get the mode of the dataset. The function will use the *unique() function* to ensure that it considers only unique values in the vector. The values are assigned to the *uniquevec variable*. We have then used *which.max() function* to perform a match in the vector values to determine which unique value occurs frequently in the dataset.

We have then created a vector of numbers and given the name y. The *getmode() function* has been invoked and the name of this vector passed to it as the argument. It will find the item that occurs most frequently within the dataset and assign it to the variable result. We have then printed the value of this variable.

Next, we have created a vector of characters and assigned it the name *charvec*. Again, we have invoked our *getmod() function* and passed the name of this vector to it as the argument. The function will find the item which occurs most frequently and assign it to the variable result. We have then printed the value of this variable.

The code should return the following result when executed:

The output shows that 1 is the mode for the numeric vector while was is the mode for the character vector.

- Data science is the process of extracting hidden patterns, trends, and relationships from data.

- R is a good programming language for performing data science tasks. It comes with many in-built functions and libraries that we can use for such tasks.

- R comes with different functions that allow us to read data stored in different file formats. Examples of such file formats include Excel, CSV, JSON, etc.

- We can use R to calculate statistical measures of a dataset. These include the mean, mode and the median.

- R does not have an in-built function for calculating the mode of data. We have to create our own function to calculate the mode of a dataset.

10 R FOR MACHINE LEARNING

In this chapter, you will the basics of machine learning and how to implement machine learning tasks in R.

Machine learning is a branch of artificial intelligence that involves the design and development of systems capable of showing an improvement in performance based on their previous experiences. This means that when reacting to the same situation, a machine should show improvement from time to time. With machine learning, software systems are able to predict accurately without having to be programmed explicitly. The goal of machine learning is to build algorithms which can receive input data then use statistical analysis so as to predict the output value in an acceptable range.

Machine learning originated from pattern recognition and the theory that computers are able to learn without the need for programming them to perform tasks. Researchers in the field of artificial intelligence wanted to determine whether computers are able to learn from data. Machine learning is an iterative approach, and this is why models are able to adapt as they are being exposed to new data. Models learn from their previous computations so as to give repeatable, reliable results and decisions.

The increasing popularity of machine learning can be attributed to the same reasons which have led to an increase in the popularity of data mining. Such factors include the availability of cheaper and powerful computational processing, availability of varieties of data and affordable means for data storage. With these, it is easy for one to quickly produce models capable of analyzing bigger and more complex data to deliver quicker and more accurate results. When an organization or business builds precise models, it becomes easy for it to identify profitable opportunities or avoid risks. With machine learning, businesses can also draw conclusions and identify patterns which can help them create models for making predictions. This can help them in making wise business decisions.

R is a great tool for machine learning. We can use it to implement a machine learning model to use any of the machine learning algorithms. In this chapter, we will demonstrate how to implement the k-Means clustering machine learning algorithm in R.

Cluster analysis falls under the category of unsupervised learning. A cluster is simply a group of data points that share similar features. Cluster analysis can be said to be more of a discovery than a prediction. The machine simply searches for similarity in the data. Here are problems on which you can apply clustering:

- Customer segmentation- this involves searching for the similarity between the groups of customers.
- Stock market clustering- this involves grouping of stocks depending on their performances.

- Dimensionality reduction in datasets by grouping the observations that have similar values.

The implementation of cluster analysis is not hard and it very applicable in businesses today. Let us use an example to demonstrate how clustering works. We will work with two dimensions to make it easy for you to understand. We will use data that shows the age of customers and their spent. We will create a plot shows the spent of the customers against their age. The plot will be created using the *ggplot2 library*. Let us import the library and load the data into a data frame:

```r
library(ggplot2)
df <- data.frame(age = c(18, 21, 22, 24, 26,
26, 27, 30, 31, 35, 39, 40, 41, 42, 44, 46,
47, 48, 49, 54),

spend = c(10, 11, 22, 15, 12, 13, 14, 33, 39,
37, 44, 27, 29, 20, 28, 21, 30, 31, 23, 24))
```

We can print the dataset by calling the name of the data frame, df:

```
> df
   age spend
1   18    10
2   21    11
3   22    22
4   24    15
5   26    12
6   26    13
7   27    14
8   30    33
9   31    39
10  35    37
11  39    44
12  40    27
13  41    29
14  42    20
15  44    28
16  46    21
17  47    30
18  48    31
19  49    23
20  54    24
>
```

The dataset has two columns, age and spend. Now, let us use the *ggplot2 library* to plot these datapoints:

```
ggplot(df, aes(x = age, y = spend)) +
geom_point()
```

The code will return the following plot:

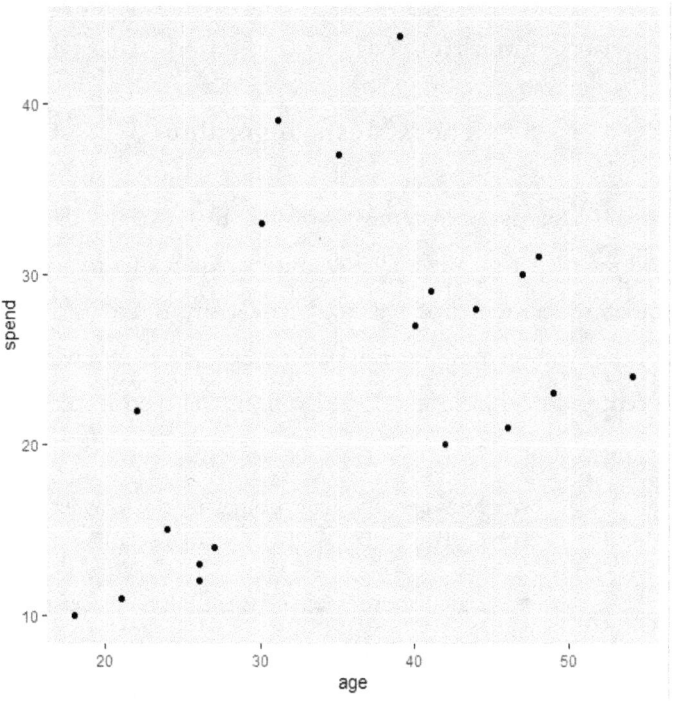

From the above plot, we can observe three patterns:

- There is a group of young people with a low purchasing power, shown on the bottom-left of the plot.

- There is a group of people aged between 30 and 40 years capable of spending more, shown on the upper middle of the plot.

- Finally, there is a group of old people, aged between 40 and 60 with a lower budget.

That is a very simple, straightforward and highly visual example. If you have a new observation, it is possible for you to tell the category under which it belongs.

The K Means Algorithm

K Means is a clustering algorithm that clusters data points based on their similarity. The algorithm requires us to specify the number of clusters that we need to classify our data into. The algorithm will then assign each data point to a cluster and calculate the centroid of the cluster. The algorithm will then iterate through two steps:

- Reassign the data points to the cluster with the closest centroid.
- Calculate the new centroid of every cluster.

The two steps given above will be repeated until the cluster variation with the cluster cannot be reduced any further. To calculate the within cluster variation, the algorithm gets the sum of Euclidian distance between the data points as well as their respective cluster centroids.

The Data

We will use the iris dataset in this chapter. This dataset comes loaded in R, so you don't have to download so as to use it. The iris dataset shows the sepal length, sepal width, petal length, and petal width of different flowers that belong to different species.

We need the first 5 rows of the dataset. First, let us load the datasets library by running the following command on the R console:

```
library(datasets)
```

We can now invoke the *head() function* to get the first 5 rows of the dataset. We should pass the name of the dataset as the argument to the function:

```
> library(datasets)
> head(iris)
  Sepal.Length Sepal.Width Petal.Length Petal.Width Species
1          5.1         3.5          1.4         0.2  setosa
2          4.9         3.0          1.4         0.2  setosa
3          4.7         3.2          1.3         0.2  setosa
4          4.6         3.1          1.5         0.2  setosa
5          5.0         3.6          1.4         0.2  setosa
6          5.4         3.9          1.7         0.4  setosa
>
```

A close observation of the dataset will reveal that the flowers belong to the same species has similar *Petal.Width* and *Petal.Length*. However, these varied considerably between species.

It will be good for us to show this visually. Let us create a plot that demonstrates this.

We will use the *ggplot2 library* to create the plot. Let us first import the library:

```
library(ggplot2)
```

We can then run the command for creating the plot:

```
ggplot(iris, aes(Petal.Length, Petal.Width,
color = Species)) + geom_point()
```

We are creating a plot of *Petal.Width* against *Petal.Length* and color the data points based on their species. This means that all data points that belong to the same species will have a similar color. The following plot will be generated:

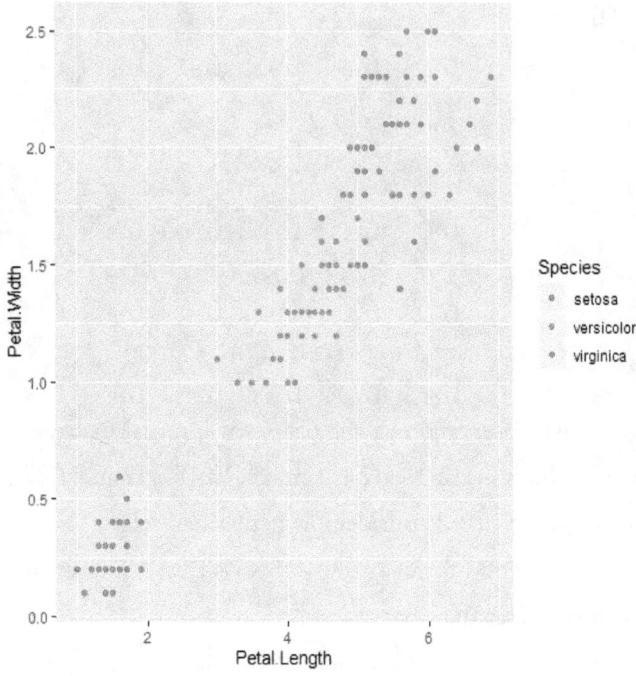

The above plot has confirmed that flowers of the same species have similar petal width and length, and this varies significantly from one species to another.

Clustering

Since you now know how the data looks like, we can go ahead and cluster it. Our first cluster assignment will be random, hence, we will set seed to ensure there is reproducibility:

```
set.seed(20)
```

We can now call the *kmeans() function* and pass the name of the dataset to it. The function will use the K Means algorithm to create clusters from the data:

```
irisCluster <- kmeans(iris[, 3:4], 3, nstart
= 20)
```

Since our dataset has three flower species, we have asked the algorithm to create 3 clusters from the dataset. Again, since we have random starting assignments, we have set *nstart = 20*. R will then choose 20 random starting assignments then choose the one that has the lowest within cluster variation. Let us now view the generated cluster, the *irisCluster*.

```
> set.seed(20)
> irisCluster <- kmeans(iris[, 3:4], 3, nstart = 20)
> irisCluster
K-means clustering with 3 clusters of sizes 50, 52, 48

Cluster means:
  Petal.Length Petal.Width
1     1.462000    0.246000
2     4.269231    1.342308
3     5.595833    2.037500

Clustering vector:
  [1] 1 1 1 1 1 1 1 1 1 1 1 1 1 1 1 1 1 1 1 1 1 1 1 1 1 1 1 1 1 1 1 1 1 1 1 1 1
 [38] 1 1 1 1 1 1 1 1 1 1 1 1 1 2 2 2 2 2 2 2 2 2 2 2 2 2 2 2 2 2 2 2 2 2 2 2 2
 [75] 2 2 2 3 2 2 2 2 2 3 2 2 2 2 2 2 2 2 2 2 2 2 2 2 2 2 3 3 3 3 3 3 2 3 3 3 3
[112] 3 3 3 3 3 3 3 3 2 3 3 3 3 3 3 2 3 3 3 3 3 3 3 3 3 3 3 2 3 3 3 3 3 3 3 3 3
[149] 3 3

Within cluster sum of squares by cluster:
[1]  2.02200 13.05769 16.29167
 (between_SS / total_SS =  94.3 %)

Available components:

[1] "cluster"      "centers"      "totss"        "withinss"     "tot.withinss"
[6] "betweenss"    "size"         "iter"         "ifault"
>
```

You can see the centroids of each cluster and the clusters to which every data point has been assigned. The within cluster variation has also been shown. We can now compare the clusters with the species:

```
table(irisCluster$cluster, iris$Species)
```

The command will return the following:

```
> table(irisCluster$cluster, iris$Species)

  setosa versicolor virginica
1     50          0         0
2      0         48         4
3      0          2        46
>
```

The above table clearly shows that data that belongs to setosa were grouped into cluster 1, versicolor into cluster 2 and virginica into cluster 3. 2 data points that belong to the versicolor and 4 data points that belong to the virginica were wrongly classified.

Let us create a plot from the data to see the clusters:

```
irisCluster$cluster <-
as.factor(irisCluster$cluster)

ggplot(iris, aes(Petal.Length, Petal.Width,
color = irisCluster$cluster)) + geom_point()
```

This will return the following plot:

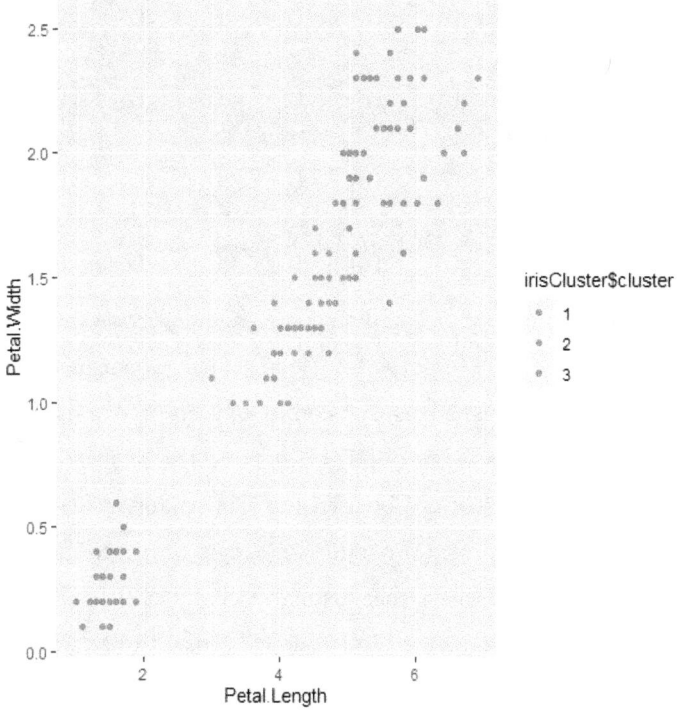

That is how the data points are distributed within the clusters.

- Machine learning is a branch of artificial intelligence in which machines such as computers show an improvement in performance based on experience.

CONCLUSION

R is a computer programming language that comes with great features. It is a good language for use in statistics, data analysis, and scientific research. The language comes with an easy to use syntax, which explains why it is a popular programming language today. R has many libraries that can be used for performing a wide range of tasks. R is an interpreted programming language, which means that there is an R interpreter rather than an R compiler. The language is available for free under the GNU public license. In R, variables are assigned with R-objects, and the data type of the R-object will become the data type of the variable. This is not the case with many other programming languages as each variable has to be defined as belonging to a particular data type.

R also supports different types of operators that we can use to perform arithmetic, relational and logical operations. The language also comes with various decision-making statements that we can use to evaluate conditions and take actions based on the outcome.

ABOUT THE AUTHOR

Daniel Bell is a computer engineer, he is conducting research in data management, with an emphasis on topics related to Big Data and data sharing, such as probabilistic data, data pricing, parallel data processing, data security. He spends his free time writing books on computer programming and data science, to help beginners in computer programming to code easily.